WRITERS WORKSHOP
FOR THE PRIMARY GRADES

ROBIN BRIGHT

PORTAGE &
MAIN PRESS

Printed and bound in Canada by Hignell Book Printing

02 03 04 05 06   5 4 3 2 1

Portage & Main Press acknowledges the financial support of the Government of Canada through the Book Publishing Industry Development Program for our publishing activities.

National Library of Canada Cataloguing in Publication Data
Bright, Robin M., 1957-
    Write from the start

    Includes bibliographical references.
    ISBN 1-895411-96-3

    1. English language–Composition and exercises–Study and teaching (Primary)
    I. Title.
LB1528.B74 2002   372.62'3044   C2002-910043-7

Book and cover design by Gallant Design Ltd.
Illustrations by Jess Dixon

PORTAGE &
MAIN PRESS

100–318 McDermot Ave.
Winnipeg, Manitoba, Canada R3A 0A2
E-mail: books@portageandmainpress.com
Tel: 1-204-987-3500
Toll-Free: 1-800-667-9673
Fax: 1-866-734-8477

For Louise, Sean, Susan, and Kerry,
my siblings, my friends

CONTENTS

ACKNOWLEDGMENTS

I would like to thank the many wonderful teachers I have worked with over the past 20 years. Their dedication to, enthusiasm for, and delight in teaching writing has benefited many children, including my own two daughters. Many teachers have inspired me to write this book. I am indebted to them for sharing with me both their successes and their challenges in teaching writing.

I would like to extend warmest thanks to my friend Faye Boer, who believes in the writing and research I do, and continues to encourage me to bring that work to teachers, parents, and students.

Finally, love and thanks go to my family, Glenn, Amy, and Erin, who provide time, space, and encouragement for me as a writer.

INTRODUCTION

Early in my career, I asked one of my colleagues what kind of support he received from other teachers and from his administrators for teaching writing. He replied, "Well, really, there's no support for teaching writing. We all pretty much do our own thing and hope we have done our best each year."

He articulated a perspective common to many educators. In the teaching of writing, teachers must develop their own instructional goals, programs, strategies, activities, and assessment procedures. Many teachers state that they are guided primarily by vague curriculum documents and government achievement tests. Yet, teaching to the test is incompatible with research and practice about how writers learn this "delicate craft." Donald Graves (1991) reminds us that students compose in idiosyncratic ways and that, while these ways seem confusing to us, we must observe the process in order to be helpful as teachers of writing. Sometimes, teachers seek certainty in their instruction by focusing on standardized practices and tests, but according to Graves this "bypasses the opportunity for child growth."

One way to develop a strong writing program is to be a careful observer of students' processes and of their writing. While teachers have access to examples of exemplary pieces of students' writing, they still ask, "What should a year-long writing program look like?" This is especially true of teachers working with the youngest students in schools, those in kindergarten, and in grades one, two, and three.

Researchers are quick to point out that much of what is known about writing and writing instruction are the results of studies conducted with older students, not those in primary classrooms. Furthermore, many researchers and curriculum writers are loathe to provide a "recipe" approach to writing. This is because the research that specifically examines students' composing processes indicates huge diversity among learners. Natalie Goldberg (1986) tells us, "Learning to write is not a linear process. There is no logical A-to-B-to-C way to become a good writer. One neat truth about writing cannot answer it all. There are many truths."

As teachers develop their programs for writing, they seek activities that are worthwhile and successful. Keeping this in mind, I have organized *Write From the Start* according to the questions teachers ask when learning about, and implementing, a new approach to teaching writing.

> Literacy is something bigger and better than mechanical skill in reading and writing. Literacy is a potent form of consciousness.
>
> —Pattison, cited in Power and Hubbard, 1991

All learners display idiosyncratic (individual) approaches to writing. Examining both the complexity of classroom writing programs and teachers' perceptions and assumptions about writing provide greater insights into effective ways of teaching writing. Taking these into consideration, the purpose of this book is to provide a wide lens through which we can view writing instruction.

Chapter 1, Wondering: What Do We Know About Writing?, provides a chance to examine recent research developments in the area of writing. In chapter 2, Listening: Perceptions and Practices, primary teachers speak about their specific challenges and successes. Chapter 3, Observing: What Writers Workshop Looks Like, provides an in-depth look at the details, routines, and plans of a writers workshop approach. In chapter 4, Applying: Promising Writing Activities, specific activities are offered to incorporate into a writers workshop approach over the course of an entire year. Chapter 5, Valuing: Responding to and Evaluating Students' Writing, provides a view of helpful, not hurtful, ways of responding to students' writing.

You may want to use the "Notes" pages following each chapter to record thoughts, feelings, ideas, and/or questions related to the reading or to highlight passages of interest. In addition, the appendices include reproducible masters for use in your writing program and in letters home to parents.

CHAPTER 1

WONDERING

WHAT DO WE KNOW ABOUT WRITING?

Writing is primarily not a matter of talent, of dedication, of vision,
of vocabulary, of style, but simply a matter of sitting.
The writer is the person who writes. — D. Murray, 1991

What can teachers do to support and encourage students who are just beginning the writing process? What is the writing process, and how can it be applied to the primary grades? Do beginning writers have specific characteristics in common? If so, what are the characteristics? These and other questions are discussed in this chapter.

A BOOK INSIDE

It has been said that everyone has a book inside; that is, we each have our own stories to tell. Some of these stories are extraordinary such as the disturbing accounts from Holocaust survivors as portrayed by author Carol Matas. Some are ordinary. For example, the stories of Stuart McLean document the experiences of a family of four—Dave, Morley, Sam, and Stephanie.

Yet, few people take the opportunity to write their own stories. Some claim they have no time, others that they have nothing to say, but most would suggest they simply could not do it. Consider that students are called upon to compose their own pieces each year for twelve years of schooling, yet most people resist the practice of lifelong writing. Teachers play a pivotal role in the enterprise of writing. Short, Harste, and Burke (1996) suggest that "How we teach writing affects what students come to believe about the writing process as well as the strategies that they use."

THE WRITING PROCESS

Fortunately, teachers have a vast amount of literature to draw upon as they consider what type of writing instruction to provide for young writers. Unfortunately, the time demands placed on teachers make it difficult for them to find and read all the literature that is available. The literature includes research devoted to writing, instructional materials, and curriculum guidelines. In the past two decades, writing instruction has been revolutionized as researchers, writers, and teachers try to define the writing process. Their attempts have resulted in a shift away from the written product and toward the process itself. For instance, when I went to school, all my writing was graded when I turned in the final copy. No one instructed me about how

When students see a book as a piece of writing, conceived and crafted by a fellow author, they begin to see themselves as writers, learning and practicing their craft.

—Skolnick, 1989

to brainstorm for ideas to write about, how to turn my ideas into a rough draft, and how to edit and polish that rough draft into a final product. Now, when I am teaching student teachers, I often have them show me their writing portfolios (a binder where they keep non-academic writing). Midway through the semester, I provide feedback and assistance during the writing process, not after it.

Currently, some agreement exists as to the nature of how people come to produce written text. Many writers appear to move through a loosely organized set of steps we have come to know as "the writing process." The steps include

1. Rehearsing (prewriting)
2. Drafting
3. Revising
4. Editing
5. Publishing

What the Steps Mean

1. **Rehearsing** occurs as students get ready to write. They brainstorm for ideas to write about. They think about their audience, their purpose for writing, and the form their writing will take (story, letter, journal entry, report, etc.).

2. **Drafting** is the process of getting ideas down on paper or on a computer screen. Expressing the ideas during this stage is paramount; spelling and punctuation will not be perfect.

3. **Revising** occurs when students read their writing aloud to themselves or to others and they see the need to change the writing. This is done by adding, deleting, moving, or otherwise changing the writing in some way.

4. **Editing** is making changes to the writing that are primarily related to conventions: spelling, punctuation, capitalization, and grammar.

5. **Publishing** is when students take their writing to a final form and read it or give it to an audience of their peers, teachers, parents, or others.

Many researchers, teachers, and writers have stressed the recursive nature of these steps in order to avoid a formulaic interpretation of the writing process. For instance, a formulaic interpretation of the writing process would have all students engage in prewriting activities (such as brainstorming or creating a chart or map of writing ideas) on Monday, writing a rough draft on Tuesday, engaging in revising activities (such as sentence combining and/or experimenting with a variety of leads) on Wednesday, editing their pieces or those of their peers on Thursday, and producing a final copy on Friday. Such an interpretation ignores the complexity of how teachers go about helping young writers. Figure 1.1 illustrates the flexibility of the writing process in a way that accommodates diversity among writers (Peterson, 1995).

Today, one would be hard-pressed to find an elementary language arts teacher who does not pay tribute to teaching the writing process in some way. Classrooms are adorned with charts listing and explaining each step in the writing process. For example, teachers say, "*Rehearsal* is a time to brainstorm or think about what to write,"

THE WRITING PROCESS

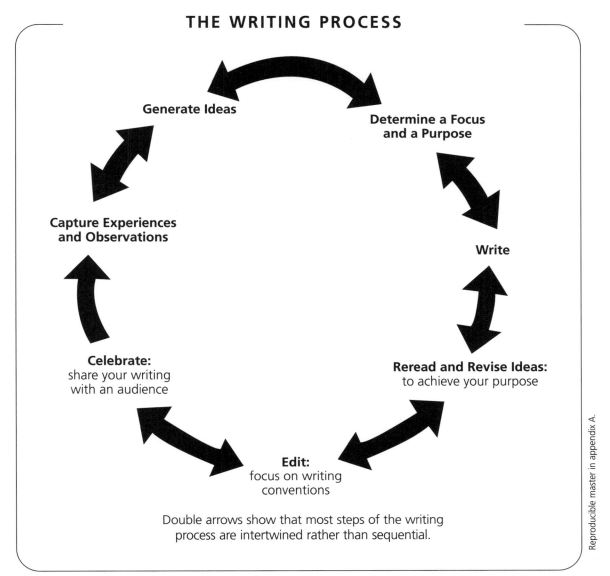

Generate Ideas

Determine a Focus and a Purpose

Capture Experiences and Observations

Write

Celebrate:
share your writing
with an audience

Reread and Revise Ideas:
to achieve your purpose

Edit:
focus on writing
conventions

Double arrows show that most steps of the writing
process are intertwined rather than sequential.

Figure 1.1. An illustration of the writing process that demonstrates flexibility and accommodation.

and "*Drafting* means getting ideas down without too much attention to spelling and punctuation, which can be examined later in the editing process," and so it goes. Furthermore, certain instructional strategies and structures are often observed in classrooms where writing is taught as process.

In spite of such wide support for teaching writing as a series of steps, occasionally we glimpse the gap that can occur between what teachers have learned about teaching writing and what actually happens in classrooms. This is particularly true when working with beginning writers. To understand students' ideas about print and writing, let us look at the features that characterize students' writing before they come to school.

Figure 1.2. Classroom bulletin boards, such as this one, review the steps of the writing process.

BEGINNING WRITERS

My daughter, Erin, produced the writing shown in figure 1.3 when she was four years old. When she showed this to me, she announced proudly, "This is you and me riding a horse, and the writing is a little song I made up." She proceeded to sing a song about riding a horse. This piece, like others produced by preschoolers, demonstrates three essential aspects of writing:

1. Intention

2. Organization

3. Experimentation (Newman, 1984)

Figure 1.3. An example of preschool writing.

STORY BOX

REAL WRITING

I observed a grade-one classroom in which the teacher was introducing journal writing to her young students. The teacher handed out notebooks and suggested that the students decorate the front cover of their writing books. The students quickly began to cut out pictures from magazines and glue these on their covers. They drew pictures and created other personal images for the books. The teacher then had them locate the first page in the notebook and asked them to write a message to her. She told her students she would write back to each of them when she took the notebooks to read. Many students began writing and drawing eagerly. I noticed scribble writing, rows of letters, pictures, and some standard words—*mom, dad, love, car*, and so on. One student, sitting close to the front of the classroom, appeared tentative about beginning. After about ten minutes, she put pencil to paper and began copying the alphabet from the long chart across the front of the room. When I asked her what she was writing, she exclaimed, "These are letters. I'm doing real writing."

INTENTION

According to Frank Smith, writing will not emerge without an underlying intention. So, what are students intending when they make marks on a page, a chalkboard, or a wall? In the beginning, one- or two-year-old children discover that their marks do not exist before putting crayon to paper. Intention lies in creating something new. Later, writing comes to represent ideas, as in the previous example of the four-year-old. For Erin, the picture and the letters demonstrate her intention to use writing to create a song. Adults can gain insight into children's intentions in their writing when those children create something and then tell us what it says or ask us to read it to them. Showing both interest in, and enthusiasm for, students' writing means taking their work seriously.

ORGANIZATION

Erin's writing also shows organization. Some aspects of its organization to consider are

- the horizontal layout of the letters
- the writing and drawing are distinguished
- the writing was produced from left to right
- the letters of her own name appear in the array of letters

When students make organizational decisions about their writing, they show their awareness of the complexity of writing. When we try to impose our own organization on their writing (by providing narrow lines to write within, for example), we make it difficult for them to figure out, on their own, how to organize their writing. We also deny them their own meaning-making strategies.

Showing both interest in, and enthusiasm for, students' writing means taking their work seriously.

EXPERIMENTATION

Finally, Erin's writing also demonstrates her ability to experiment. She has experimented with format, letter formation, and meaning. Even several weeks after producing this piece, when I asked her what she wrote, she replied, "Remember, I said it is a song." She proceeded to sing a song that differed from the original, but still maintained the horse-riding theme. Experimentation is essential to learning about language. One prominent researcher writes:

> Students need to be able to experiment with what they want to say, to whom they want to say it, and how they want to say it. They need to experiment with form and format, spelling and punctuation...Yet if no risks are taken, little can be learned (Newman, 1984).

CHARACTERISTICS OF WRITING

In addition to understanding how beginning writers approach writing in the first place, we must also consider what we know about the enterprise of writing. There are two major characteristics of writing:

1. Writing as distinct and personal
2. Writing as a developmental process

WRITING AS DISTINCT AND PERSONAL

Writing is one area of the language arts curriculum that defies a model of organization that fits all classrooms or all students. The majority of teachers I know say they use an "eclectic" approach to teaching writing, pulling ideas and activities from various sources. Some teachers teach writing based on previous teaching experiences. They design a program and establish classroom practice through trial and error. Others follow a specific program, building on patterned and structured activities. Still, another group of teachers approach writing instruction in a way that falls somewhere between the other two approaches. While many teachers credit the writing process movement (promoted by teacher researchers like Donald Graves and Nancie Atwell) with improving their writing instruction, many of these same teachers continue to articulate frustrations about teaching writing. They wonder about whether or not they are really providing instruction that improves the writer and the writing:

I am not sure if my students understand the concept of writing a story. I do think my better readers have a better understanding.
> —Grade-one teacher

My efforts (in writing instruction) have been sporadic. I don't exactly know the correct steps I should be following. I think there should be some sequence to it so that if I try this, then this, that they are going to get it.
> —Grade-one teacher

The most frustrating part of teaching writing is not having the time to go through the whole process of the writing process every time you do it.

—Grade-two teacher

The most frustrating area is what you do after it (the piece) is written. The editing—this handy little resource that I'm reading says it's only supposed to take five or six minutes per student—but I talk half an hour with one student.

—Grade-three teacher

My own experience as a grade-one teacher and as a parent of two students suggests that writing is as individual as the students themselves. Teachers know this. During the first month of school in grade one, a teacher is likely to see samples of writing that vary in length, use of space, uppercase letters and punctuation, and creativity. At this age, students exhibit a wide range in spelling ability and fine motor coordination. Since teachers face tremendous diversity among their young students, how can they begin the task of teaching writing in a way that meets that diversity? The examples shown in figure 1.4 demonstrate two writing samples produced in a grade-one classroom during the first month of school.

Figure 1.4. Grade-one writing samples produced during the first month of school.

Writing comprises ineffable qualities and can be an intensely personal and distinctive act. For instance, many of us recognize who penned a letter or memo—not by the signature, but by the words used, the grammatical structures, the tone, and other attributes. While teachers can give instruction in grammar, vocabulary, spelling, handwriting, and paragraphing, how these things come together for a writer is highly distinctive. Frank Smith describes writing as "a highly personal and emotionally charged activity" (Smith, 1982).

WRITING AS A DEVELOPMENTAL PROCESS

The importance of writing during the early years is, according to many teachers, a "breakthrough" understanding in the area of writing knowledge and instruction. Several prominent researchers agree. Elbow (1993) writes: "Very young students can learn to write before they can read. Thus, writing naturally precedes reading." (See also Hillocks, 1986; Atwell, 1999; and Teale and Sulzby, 1986.)

Many primary teachers agonize about the best way to help young writers. Knowing there is a developmental continuum for preschool writing can be helpful when looking at, and wondering about, how best to work with young students as writers. The continuum, shown in figure 1.5, depicts milestones to watch for in young students' writing.

DEVELOPMENTAL CONTINUUM FOR PRESCHOOL WRITING

Before age 3: Children produce mostly random scribbling.

Around age 3: Children begin to understand some of the things that writing is used for (e.g., "This is a letter for Grandma," or "I've written a list of things to buy when we go shopping").

Some children also begin to understand that writing consists of letter-like formations (although they can't necessarily name the letters produced).

Around age 4: Students' awareness of letters becomes more specific. For instance, students can often name letters in their own names or point out the big letter *M* for McDonald's.

After producing letters, they will often tell another person what it says. There will likely be no attempt to sound out the letters. However, what they have written may look like a story or a message. Some students will bring their "writing" to an adult and ask, "What does it say?"

Between ages 5 and 7: This is the time when students discover that print represents the sounds of words. Some students make this discovery in kindergarten. Other students are not aware that print represents the sounds of words until well into grade one.

It is important to keep in mind that although students first produce scribbles, pictures, and letters, their understanding proceeds from sentences, to words, and finally to letters. Their scribbles can be used to represent any of these (Casbergue, 1998).

Reproducible master in appendix B.

Figure 1.5. Developmental continuum for preschool writing.

WHAT WRITERS SAY ABOUT THEIR WRITING

Sara Ellis, author of several children's books, made up stories all the time as part of her play, yet she writes: "I never once thought that these imaginings had anything to do with the kind of stories you wrote down. When I was asked to write a story in school, I didn't have a single idea."

C. S. Lewis writes: "All I can tell you is that pictures come into my head and I write stories about them." Other famous quotes highlight writing as a discovery process:

> I write because I don't know what I think until I read what I say.
>
> O'Connor, cited in Murray, 1990

> How do I know what I think until I see what I say?
>
> E. M. Forster, cited in Murray, 1990

> I have to write every day because, the way I work, the writing generates the writing.
>
> Doctorow, cited in Murray, 1990

These diverse comments suggest that no two writers are the same. Some writers go so far as to say that learning to write is a process of "uneducation" rather than education. As a result, it is not surprising that teachers sometimes do not know where to start. Consider two young students in a grade-one class who recently began writing in their new journals. One began her journal with "Dr Techr" (Dear Teacher) and continued with a short message about herself. The other student examined the alphabet hung across the front of the classroom and began to copy the letters into her journal. These young writers remind us that classroom routines, procedures, and teaching strategies need to reflect the diversity among young writers. Teachers need to provide the kind of writing environment that encourages students to start writing (drawing and/or scribbling), using structures they are comfortable with. From there, mini-lessons, teacher demonstrations, and feedback are offered so that students' writing processes are highlighted. Final written products, though important, should not overshadow the students' desire to develop their ideas and learn to be at ease with the process of writing.

A CAUTIONARY NOTE

After listening to teachers talk about teaching writing in the early grades, we need to remind ourselves that the writing process is a fluid and recursive cycle. It should not be interpreted as a set of sequential steps to lock a student's piece of writing into. Such an interpretation tends to make writing appear static, rigid, and easy to accomplish. Others have called this an "assembly-line picture" of the authoring cycle. It is important to avoid this interpretation, particularly in the primary grades. It can be detrimental for teachers and students to believe that writing must always follow a prescribed series of steps. Such interpretations cause us to become frustrated by our inability to help every student produce a near-perfect piece of writing.

An assembly-line picture of the writing process occurs when teachers spend invaluable time planning writing activities so that their students experience and become knowledgeable about the various steps of the process. Less time is spent actually writing, thinking about one's writing, and improving one's writing. In some classrooms, students are required or advised to follow a methodical and sequential step-by-step process as they attend to a writing task. It goes something like this: On Monday, students experience a prewriting activity by reading a story, brainstorming, or going on a field trip. On Tuesday and Wednesday, students draft their ideas on paper. They may be encouraged to put their ideas down quickly (double-spaced to make revisions easier) and to leave mechanics until later. Thursday is devoted to revising: does it make sense to me, to others? Does it need to be changed? Editing comes next. This is when attention is given to the mechanics of writing—capitalization, punctuation, and spelling. And if the students hang in there until Friday, they can publish their writing, usually by recopying it to another format (computer, booklet, photocopied paper, and so on). If I were forced into a predetermined schedule of process and skill as just described, I would not write much at all.

Teachers must somehow achieve a balance between developing fluency in writing and providing instruction in spelling, grammar, punctuation, vocabulary, and other necessary skills. Primary teachers must place a greater emphasis on providing uninterrupted time for writing and for talking about writing. How best to provide that time and how to structure it to benefit all students is the focus of the rest of this book. I have combined my research to develop a writers workshop approach and promising practices for early writing instruction.

SUMMARY

- How we teach writing affects what students come to believe about the writing process, as well as what strategies they use.

- Writers appear to move through a loosely organized set of steps known as the writing process—rehearsing, drafting, revising, editing, and publishing.

- Beginning writers demonstrate intention, organization, and experimentation in their scribbles/drawing/writing.

- Writing, as a curriculum area, is both personal and developmental: teachers face tremendous diversity among their young students.

NOTES

NOTES

CHAPTER 2

LISTENING

PERCEPTIONS AND PRACTICES

...engaging in reflections about their own practices, then sharing their experiences with other professionals, helped teachers to continually expand their own thinking about their teaching. — Hiebert and Raphael, 1998

This chapter focuses on teachers' perceptions of writing instruction in the primary grades. Specifically, teachers talk about two frustrating aspects of their practice— lack of time and convincing students of the importance of the revision habit. They also share those guiding principles that seem beneficial to their students' development as writers.

WHY STUDY PRIMARY WRITING INSTRUCTION?

As a professor of education, I have opportunities to visit many classrooms and speak to primary teachers about writing instruction. To more fully explore and document primary writing instruction, I wanted to hear from teachers about their practices and perceptions of teaching writing. I developed and sent out an in-depth survey to 294 teachers of grades K-3. I asked teachers to characterize their writing programs and to document their frustrations about teaching writing, as well as both their most successful and least successful teaching practices (see appendix C for the complete survey). I also observed several primary classrooms in order to fully document teaching practices and, in some cases, students' perceptions of those practices. I hoped that by working with teachers and students in the classroom setting, I could (a) shed light on successful primary writing instruction and (b) offer these to other teachers in the form of lessons, or what I call "Promising Writing Activities."

In all, I collected 115 teacher survey forms, observed many hours of classroom teaching, and reviewed more than 90 pieces of students' writing samples. The voices of the teachers with whom I worked provide the backbone of this book. As teachers and researchers continue to describe aspects of the classroom context that appear beneficial to writing growth in students, new strategies for instruction may become evident.

What Primary Teachers Say

In this chapter, the teachers' responses are organized around two main survey questions:

1. What frustrates you about teaching writing?

2. What are your most successful activities for teaching writing?

These questions focus attention on the characteristics of classrooms where teachers consistently work to improve writing instruction, while they acknowledge the difficulties in doing so.

What Frustrates Primary Teachers About Writing Instruction?

Two main themes emerged as teachers wrote and talked to me about their writing instruction:

1. The lack of time to devote to meeting students' individual needs as writers.

2. The inability to work effectively with young students on revising their writing.

Lack of Time

The following quote encapsulates the overwhelming response from surveyed teachers:

> *I find it frustrating to know how to work with each student individually to "develop" his or her stories. The whole idea of editing, conferencing, first drafts, second drafts, and how to do it effectively with one teacher and thirty students, especially in grade one, is very frustrating.*
> —Grade-two teacher

...the teacher often does not have the time to meet an individual student's learning needs at precisely the moment when it is needed.

Many teachers point to the lack of time they have to spend with individual students on their writing. They recognize the importance of providing instruction in writing that is timely and purposeful. For example, when a student attempts to sound out the word *then* and writes "zen," a teacher wants to talk to that student, at that moment, about words that begin with *th*. However, the teacher often does not have the time to meet an individual student's learning needs at precisely the moment when it is needed. And so, asks the teacher, how can I set up and organize writing instruction so that both my time and the students' time are used productively? Figure 2.1 offers ideas for managing time effectively in a writers workshop.

By implanting a writers workshop approach into the teaching of writing, students—even the youngest in schools—learn to be both independent and fluent as writers. This allows teachers more time to work with students individually and in small groups.

Revising

Revising is another aspect of the writing process that confuses and frustrates teachers of young students. One teacher expressed these feelings: "Not having enough time to work individually with students in the revising stage is frustrating. Often students are reluctant to go beyond the initial drafting stage in the publishing process." It is clear that teachers need to be consulted as to the practical aspects of

PRINCIPLES FOR MANAGING TIME

1. Encourage students to develop fluency in their writing by helping them to seek out "standard" spellings on word walls, in their individualized spelling books, and from peers.

2. Encourage students to draw pictures, use scribble lines, or sound out the words when they use vocabulary in their writing that cannot be found in those places listed in #1. For example, a student trying to write the word *especially*, might write "espvvvv" or "esphsle."

3. Keep track of individual student's writing progress by developing a "tracking" sheet. At the beginning of writers workshop, students place their names under the appropriate headings—prewriting, drafting, revising/editing, publishing, conferencing—to indicate what they are working on that day.

4. Develop routines that students can carry out on their own. For example, student helpers distribute writing folders during recess or at lunch. Students assemble themselves on a carpeted area of the classroom in preparation for the mini-lesson that begins writers workshop.

Reproducible master in appendix D.

Figure 2.1. Principles for Managing Time.

teaching writing. Their insights and experiences can inform the theory underlying the writing curriculum.

Here are what several primary teachers say specifically about revising:

*   Students want their rough copy to be the only copy they have to do.

*   Students want to stick with what they first write.

*   Students don't see the value in adding or deleting words or phrases.

*   Students who write well seem to get tired and have abrupt endings.

*   Students aren't interested in revising their work. Some would rather just start a new story.

*   Students don't come up with many questions or revision ideas when working with a peer.

*   There is a tendency to let the teacher find what needs to be revised.

One grade-three teacher wrote:

> *Rarely do they want to go and change anything, you know, to make this the best possible writing it could be. I find that they have ownership of a piece right up until the first draft is done. Then, it's done! I find that a huge hurdle.*

…actual revisions made are less important than the "habit" of reviewing one's writing.

These comments tell us that young students should first focus on fluency and independence in writing. While the teacher models revision and editing habits with mini-lessons, the actual revisions made are less important than the *habit* of reviewing one's writing. Interestingly, a particular revision may actually make the writing worse. Several suggestions regarding what to do about revision emerged from the data (see figure 2.2).

PRINCIPLES FOR REVISING

1. Focus on helping students engage in writing for real purposes. One example of this is the "sign-in" routine (Richgels, 1996). Kindergarten students learn the value of writing by signing an attendance page each day. The routine help them to practice and experiment with letter shape and size, spelling, and with viewing other's efforts.

2. Focus mostly on drafting during the writing process. This allows students to develop fluency and independence.

3. Teach the *habit* of revising as much as the *actual* revision. Researchers call this "monitoring their own writing behaviors" and suggest students do this when they are encouraged to be active in learning (Askew and Fountas, 1998).

4. Judge each revision situation according to the student. Since it is unlikely that any writer attempts to revise all aspects of a piece of writing at one time, it does not make sense for a student to do this. As a rule of thumb, limit the student's number of revisions to between three and five on a single page (depending on the student's ability to handle these).

Reproducible master in appendix E.

Figure 2.2. Principles for Revising.

SUCCESSFUL ACTIVITIES FOR TEACHING WRITING

In the survey, the majority of teachers indicated the importance of combining theory and practice to create a successful writing program. In theory, teachers talked about the principle of being able to acknowledge and accept young students' writing when they first come to school. In practice, writers workshop was discussed by approximately 70 percent of the teachers as a worthwhile approach to organizing writing instruction.

In Theory

Before coming to school, students engage in many activities that could be characterized as writing. They scribble on a chalkboard, paint on newsprint, and draw on paper (figure 2.3).

Many students believe they are writing as they create their story pictures. As a teacher of young writers, it is necessary to say, in response to their creations, "Tell me about your writing." Then, students are encouraged to add letters to represent the story.

Figure 2.3. Writing samples created by preschoolers.

In Practice

Teachers have read and heard about setting up a writers workshop in their classrooms; many have experimented with this approach to instruction. For instance, they set aside regular time periods for writing, teach skills during mini-lessons, and engage students in conferences about their writing.

However, while many teachers are convinced of the usefulness of using writers workshop in their classrooms, they are unsure about how to implement such an approach. A teacher may ask: How should the classroom be organized? Will I lose control of my students? What does the first day or month of writers workshop look like? How will I teach the skills I need to teach?

So, in theory and in practice, primary teachers identify what they consider to be important aspects of writing instruction.

Students learn to improve their writing when the following characteristics are evident:

- Writing is used for real purposes.
- The focus for writing is on developing fluency and independence.
- Drawing, writing, and scribbling are acknowledged as genuine writing and communication.
- Social interaction is encouraged as they develop plans for writing.
- Text generation is not separate from planning.
- They have uninterrupted periods of time for writing.

These characteristics represent a sound teaching approach to writing without being overly prescriptive. This is important in a discipline that acknowledges and values diversity among learners.

In general, educators know a great deal about teaching writing. They create lessons to fit the needs of their students and modify those same lessons when they do not work.

They sometimes feel free to allow students to develop as writers in creative ways. Other times, they feel constrained by the classroom context—timetables, curriculum, standardized tests, administrative demands—in a way that makes it

Set aside regular time periods for writing, teach skills during mini-lessons, and engage students in conferences about their writing.

difficult for young writers to develop successfully. Overall, they see great variation among students and talk about how to develop a well-defined writing curriculum for their students.

The next two chapters offer a well-developed, yet flexible, curriculum for writing in the primary grades based on the above-mentioned characteristics. The descriptions and lessons represent what many have come to understand about teaching writing to the youngest members of our schools. The ideas are intended to be used as a guide, not as a mandate, in classrooms. As always, new teaching ideas should be considered in light of the following questions:

- Does it work?
- Does it make sense?
- Does it last? (Atwell, 1999)

SUMMARY

- Teachers talk specifically about the frustrations and successes associated with teaching writing in the primary grades.

- Two areas that primary teachers find frustrating are lack of time to teach writing and revising as a skill for young students.

- Primary teachers balance the need to devise a writing curriculum and custom-fit their instruction to students' individual writing processes.

- Primary teachers identify what they consider to be important aspects of writing instruction—purpose, fluency, independence, acknowledgement, social interaction.

NOTES

NOTES

CHAPTER 3

OBSERVING

WHAT WRITERS WORKSHOP LOOKS LIKE

The authoring cycle is our attempt to make curriculum visible to both teachers and students. It connects theory and practice, supports planning, and predicts teaching by providing a framework to guide instructional decision-making. It provides us with a structure, not a sequence, for our work together in classrooms.
— Short, Harste, and Burke, 1996

This chapter introduces and describes writers workshop as an instructional approach that helps students and teachers see themselves as storytellers and writers. It addresses the how-to of beginning and maintaining a writers workshop in kindergarten through grade three. Many practical aspects of writers workshop are addressed, including the physical classroom set-up, timetables, and important routines.

WHY WRITERS WORKSHOP?

Primary teachers' responses to the questions, "What frustrates you about teaching writing?" and "What are your most successful activities for teaching writing?" indicated they want an approach to writing instruction that

- allows students to write for real purposes
- focuses on developing fluency and independence in writing
- actively engages young students in creating texts

This section is devoted to looking at ways of developing and maintaining a writers workshop approach in the classroom. Many teachers who were surveyed said they felt they were more successful encouraging young students to write when they used writers workshop in their classrooms. For others, the term *writers workshop* conjured up images of chaos, disorganization, and noise. To gain insight into the potential benefits and pitfalls of using a writers workshop approach, perhaps the best place to begin is by engaging in a short exercise. Using the chart in figure 3.1, brainstorm and record all the words that come to mind when you think of the following two environments: classroom and workshop.

Now look at your two lists. What do you notice? Does anything surprise you when you look at your lists? Chances are you have discovered that there are positive and negative aspects to both of these environments. I asked a group of elementary teachers to do this exercise recently. One remarked how surprised she was to see that she came up with so many positive attributes associated with a workshop environment; she had always avoided this type of instructional approach. Her adjectives included: *working hard, intense, independent,* and *creative.*

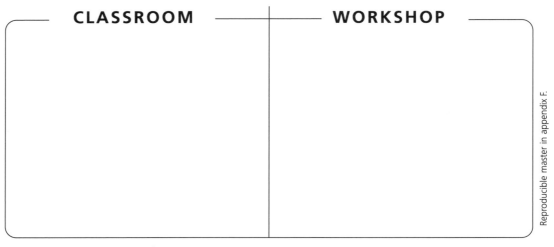

CLASSROOM **WORKSHOP**

Figure 3.1. Brainstorming chart.

Any of these adjectives could also be applied to a classroom environment. More often than not, however, they turn up when brainstorming about a workshop environment. Seldom do words such as *unstructured, chaotic,* or *undirected* appear on the workshop list. This comes as a surprise to those who see a workshop model in that way.

Yet, workshop approaches depend on highly structured environments and on constant talk about good writing. Several teachers in the study offered the following perspective:

> *I believe in and practice writers workshop. It is an approach that can be used effectively from grade one through to university. The PROCESS is what is MOST important. Students enjoy this approach, quickly become involved in writing, and show growth over time. Students take responsibility for selecting their writing topics and deciding on which area they will work on.*

Other research describing characteristics of exemplary first-grade literacy instruction tells us that teachers use writers workshop as a means for students to select and write about topics that interest them (Morrow, Tracey, and Pressley, 1999).

Because of teachers' perceptions, it is important to examine how to manage writing instruction using a writers workshop approach in the primary grades.

THE ART OF TELLING A STORY

Writers workshop is a place to tell and to listen to stories. These stories can be told and repeated, and they can be read from literature.

I receive several requests from primary teachers each fall to do demonstration lessons related to writers workshop. "How do you start the whole thing?" they ask, or, "Should I wait until November to really begin writing?" The most requested demonstration lesson is what Nancie Atwell (1997) calls, "Getting Started," and Donald Graves (1982) calls, "Day One." It is not that primary teachers are uninformed about this approach to writing instruction. Rather, they are all too familiar with the writing process—prewriting, drafting, revising, editing, and publishing. They ask for a demonstration so they can observe someone, actually implement a workshop approach to instruction. They then know what expectations they should have for themselves and for their students.

Teachers' questions include: "What should I expect students to write about? Do they need lots of help coming up with topics? How do I orchestrate routines when students are involved in different aspects of the writing process simultaneously? Will my classroom be chaotic? What do I say to them to get them started?" On my office wall is a quote. I reread it whenever I am thinking about what it means to be a writer and how to encourage others to think about this as well. It says:

> Students want to write. They want to write the first day they attend school. This is no accident. Before they went to school they marked up walls, pavements, newspapers with crayons, chalk, pens or pencils... anything that makes a mark. The student's marks say, "I am."
>
> —Graves, 1982

How to Begin

The following sections provide ideas for introducing and organizing writers workshop over several weeks and beyond. These ideas are presented as follows:

- The First Week—Telling Stories
- The Second Week—More Stories and Introducing Routines
- The Third Week—Talking About Writers and Writing
- The Fourth Week—Writing and Conferencing
- Maintaining a Writers Workshop Classroom

I know many primary teachers who schedule writers workshop on Tuesday and Thursday afternoons for one hour each day and others who have students write on Monday, Wednesday, and Friday for about thirty minutes each day. Timetable decisions are best made in conjunction with students' needs and interests.

The First Week—Telling Stories

During the first week, model storytelling by telling short (one to three minutes each) stories about everyday happenings such as walking to school, playing with a pet, playing a soccer game, or going to the park. Storytelling occurs at the beginning of writers workshop and lasts five to fifteen minutes, depending on the students' interest.

After the storytelling, say, "Now any one of these makes a good story to write about because it happened to me, and I have no trouble remembering or writing about something that is so close to me." Then ask, "Do you have some stories to tell about things, just ordinary things, that have happened to you or someone you know?" The students often respond eagerly and tell one another stories that they recall. After about ten minutes, and after each student has had an opportunity to tell at least one story to another person, ask them to tell you what their stories were about. "My story is about the time I got lost in the department store." Or, "Mine is when my family eats a big dinner at Grandma's and I always eat too much." Another might say, "My story is about moving because this is my last day of school." After each comment, respond with something like, "Wow! You have a story to tell, don't you!" Sharing like this continues for a few minutes until you sense the students' enthusiasm for their topics. Then, say, "Let's write down our stories so that we can share them with each other." It is time to write.

STORY BOX

DAY ONE

I recently visited a grade-three classroom in a rural community, at the request of the classroom teacher. The teacher asked if I would get her students started writing. She wanted me to use a writers workshop format that she could continue throughout the school year. Feeling a little nervous, but excited about working with a group of eight- and nine-year olds interested in writing, I ventured out. The students had been primed for my visit and seemed eager to see what was on the morning's agenda.

After saying good morning to the class and showing them my writing book (a messy-looking pink notebook with a coil spine and containing some 200 pages), I recounted everything I had done that morning in order to arrive at their school at the appointed time. The school, located about one hour's traveling time from my home, meant that I had a few, albeit mundane, stories to tell when I arrived. I started by saying simply, "When I woke up this morning, I knew I was coming to your school to do some writing, so I started thinking about what I might write about with you today." I continued, "My morning began with a bang! The alarm clock had gone off at the right time but my husband, seeing his family sleeping so soundly, decided to give us a few extra minutes and so left us quietly to pursue our deep sleep dreams. Well, the next thing I knew, my ten-year-old daughter was crying over my bed that she was going to be late for school, and why hadn't someone woken her up earlier! We managed to get everyone dressed and fed before school, and I don't think she was late." I told them, "Then, while I was having my breakfast of cereal and orange juice, I looked over at the calendar that hangs on the refrigerator and noticed a beautiful scene right over the month of September. It was mountain scenery and showed a tall, rugged-looking mountain covered with snow at the top, lots of green and brown fir trees in the foreground, and a calm-looking stream flowing in and out of the trees. Fortunately, the picture had a calming effect on me, considering the hectic start to the day. I began thinking that maybe I could write about a place like the one in the picture. I wondered what might happen there that I could write about and then I stopped. I realized that I did not spend much time in the mountains, and it would be hard for me to write about a place that I did not know much about. So, I decided that I probably would not write about the mountains." ▶

I had just modeled what does *not* make a good topic for writing. Writers need to write, I said, about what they know so their writing is believable and so that their own voices come through. I told the students another story that had occurred to me sometime before that morning. I explained that what makes it a good story is that I have heard myself tell this story over and over again to many different people. So, I told this group of grade-three students one of my favorite stories. It took approximately three to four minutes to tell the story. You can read the story in the next story box.

THE SECOND WEEK—MORE STORIES AND INTRODUCING ROUTINES

During week two of writers workshop, continue to tell and listen to students' stories. Many students return to school the day after being introduced to writers workshop armed with new ideas for writing—they have been "on the alert" for ideas and experiences to write about. Encourage students to write about themselves, their experiences, and their world—even though it may take some time. We all know students who return from a family holiday from a place like Disneyland and write in their journal: "I went to Disneyland. I had fun." Even students who have out-of-the-ordinary experiences cannot write about them unless they have been taught to value all experiences as worthwhile writing material. So, they ask, "What about sleeping over at my cousin's house? Could I write about that?" and "I helped make supper last night. I'm going to write about that." On a more serious note, some students want to write about experiencing "lockdown" procedures in their schools and other difficult issues as a way of trying to understand the challenges facing students today.

Provide students with uninterrupted time for writing, and begin to establish routines for writers workshop. One example of how to organize writers workshop is as follows:

To Begin

- Ask students to meet together on a carpeted area of the classroom.

- Give a short (five-minute) mini-lesson on developing ideas for writing (see pages 39–40), and talk about writing folders (see pages 40–42)—what they look like, how and where they will be stored, and expectations for behavior during writing time.

- In the beginning, you may not wish to meet with students (either individually or in small groups) for too long at a time, but prefer to manage the group as a whole. This ensures classroom management does not become a problem, because you are is able to oversee that students understand the routines and expectations.

Writing Time

- After the mini-lesson, students use the majority of the time for writing.

- Some teachers begin by giving students approximately fifteen minutes of uninterrupted time for writing. Gradually increase that time to forty-five minutes and then to one hour after several months of writers workshop.

STORY BOX

TELLING STORIES

My husband and I used to live on an acreage just outside the town where we now live. One reason we moved to the acreage was to be able to have several animals and let them roam free. So, within a couple of months, we acquired our new family: Panther, a black kitten, Ginger, a white and reddish-colored pup, and Buck, a huge, honey-colored golden retriever. Not long after we moved there, I was at home alone for the night. My husband traveled sometimes for work, and he stayed in places like Miami, Los Angeles, and Seattle. I was happy to be home on the acreage taking care of our rambunctious "family." I felt pretty safe because I had, I figured, three wonderful pets to protect me. This particular evening, I went to bed around 11:00 p.m. I was awakened from a deep sleep around one o'clock in the morning. What had awakened me I couldn't really say, but as I lay in my bed I thought I heard voices downstairs. Pretty strange, I thought. Even more strange, however, was that my fearless protectors (Panther, Ginger, and Buck) were not anywhere in sight. I didn't want to call them since I could still hear the muffled voices coming from below. Finally, I ventured down the stairs ever so quietly and slowly. On the one hand, I admired my courage. On the other hand, I was scared to death. I tiptoed through the hallway next to the family room where the voices seemed to be coming from. I could even see a light on in the room. I approached the doorway to the room and peeked around the corner, not knowing what I would see. And then, when my eyes focused on what was there, I started to laugh and I mean, really laugh. Before me, three animals were watching a movie on the large-screen television. Buck's right paw was placed firmly on the remote control. I realized he had inadvertently placed his paw there and turned the television on. When I finally stopped laughing, I took the remote away from Buck. As I placed it up on a shelf, I vowed never to let that happen again!

Listening to Others

Another useful routine is to gather students together for the last five to ten minutes of writers workshop. Encourage listening by having students read their writing aloud. It is important, in these initial writers workshop sessions, to set up routines that you and the students are comfortable with and that can be anticipated each time you engage in writers workshop.

THE THIRD WEEK—TALKING ABOUT WRITERS AND WRITING

Young students engage in writing because they have something to communicate. The first hurdle is to help them trust that what they know and have to say is important enough to write down. This can be difficult for some students, and a teacher can sometimes spend several months or even an entire year working on this idea alone. For many other students, once they trust their stories and write on a fairly consistent basis, they are ready for a supportive adult to work with them on their writing.

Teachers do this in many ways. One way is to bring in exemplary literature (trade books that are characterized by high standards in writing and/or illustration) to read to students during writers workshop or at other times during the day.

Exemplary children's literature can be used as the basis for mini-lessons on writing. Depending on the learner outcomes for the lesson, focus on

- vocabulary
- illustrations
- technique
- point of view
- characters

- setting
- plot
- beginnings
- form
- foreshadowing

- style
- endings
- dialogue
- mood

S T O R Y   B O X
U S I N G   L I T E R A T U R E

In a grade-three class, the teacher reads *Josepha* by Jim McGugan. Students close their eyes and imagine a scene from the story as she reads:

It was late in the last afternoon, long after the school bell, when I made good-byes to Josepha. Prairie wind ruffled his hair. Barefoot, he stood silent and still as a Saturday flagpole. The sun flickered between leaves in the windbreak poplars, licking his face in shadow and light. Shadow and light. And a farm cart's four wheels groaned and whined not far down the gravel track. A farm cart coming for Josepha.

The students tell the teacher what words helped to describe the scene they imagined. The teacher records the words on chart paper and teaches students to use words that describe an object, a place, or a person.

Another approach is to use the student's own writing as a starting point for teaching about writing. Ask a student to read aloud his or her draft piece and, with the class, comment positively about specific writing strategies used. For example, ask, "Could you read your first line and tell us why you started your story that way?" (Ask students privately if they would like to read their writing aloud in this way.)

During week three of writers workshop, the teacher helps students talk about what writers do. This type of talk continues throughout the year with students often providing their observations about writers and writing.

Norman Pite, a grade-five/six teacher talks with students about issues and topics that they struggle with. Working with Donald, Norman offers some tips on spelling. He suggests that Donald continue writing and then go back later to identify and fix spelling. When working with Jaime, a gifted sixth-grade writer, Norman suggests that she think of writing as climbing a mountain, "You are at the top of a mountain now as a writer. But, as you gaze around, you see a taller mountain in the distance and you want to climb that mountain. To get there, you must go down the mountain you are on—take some steps backward—before you can go forward and climb the new mountain."

The kind of talk the teacher engages in depends on the student and on his or her needs and interests as a writer.

STORY BOX

TEACHING DIALOGUE

In a combination grade two/three class, the teacher has asked a student, who is beginning to use dialogue in his writing, if it is all right to print the story on chart paper so that everyone can see the story. The story goes:

Once upon a time, a Queen lived in a castle with her two daughters.
One day she said It's too hot inside this dreary castle.

The teacher, using the student's own writing sample, showed this student and the rest of the class how to punctuate dialogue. The writing lesson is meaningful to this student and others who are using dialogue or thinking about using dialogue in their writing.

THE FOURTH WEEK—WRITING AND CONFERENCING

By now, students are familiar with the routines of writers workshop. At this point, they would benefit from one-on-one and small-group feedback while they are engaged in their writing. A teacher colleague recently commented to me that she believes most of us give "impoverished responses" to students' writing. While time affects our responses, so too do the routines of writers workshop. By waiting to introduce conferencing with students, until they feel comfortable and somewhat independent as writers, teachers will be more successful with classroom management during conferencing. The following steps show how to begin the routine of conferencing:

1. Ask students to sign their names on the board, or another appointed place, to show that they are ready to meet with you individually about a piece of writing.

2. Call together small groups of students whose writings show similarities, so that a small-group conference is beneficial to all.

3. Use a combination of the previous two methods.

Establishing an effective system of conferencing helps you teach the "writer," as opposed to teaching the "writing." Teaching the writing occurs when teachers mark a student's writing and returns it with a grade and a comment. Grading and returning a student's writing provides no opportunity for the teacher to teach the writer.

It is important to have several weeks' worth of storytelling and student writing (three to five draft pieces) before asking students to work in another stage of the writing process. I have made the mistake of allowing students to write only one piece and then moving that piece through all the stages of the writing process. By doing so, I took away the two most important aspects of writing—ownership and choice. If students have several pieces from which to choose, they are able to exercise freedom of choice in the piece that becomes important to them over a period of time. Many of us would not want to spend two weeks working on a piece of writing that does not interest us. On the other hand, we will spend hours on something that intrigues and captures our attention.

STORY BOX
A DAY AT HOME

The grade-one teacher asks four students to come together at a circular table in the back of the classroom. She asks these four student to join her today because, as she tells them,

Each of you has written about what it is like to be at home during the day on a weekend. Your stories are very interesting and very different, because each of you is unique and has unique experiences. Today, while we listen to each story, see if you can tell us something that is unique about that person, based on what that person has written about.

In this way, the teacher gives students a purpose for listening to one another and helps them to see both the similarities and the differences that arise when students write on topics of their own choosing.

MAINTAINING A WRITERS WORKSHOP CLASSROOM

How writers workshop evolves depends upon both the teacher's interests and the students' interests.

THEMES

Many primary teachers organize their instruction around major topics or themes. This permits an integrated approach in which many curriculum areas can be addressed. For example, a unit on insects meets curriculum objectives in language arts (with the literature of E. McCarle), science, mathematics, and even art.

Teachers may find that students are anxious to use writers workshop as a place to do more writing and reading about a topic or theme they are studying. Their stories and reports, when thematically based, can be richer in description as they make use of new knowledge derived from several different subject areas. Writers workshop permits students to write about topics and themes they are studying, and to choose a format that appeals to them.

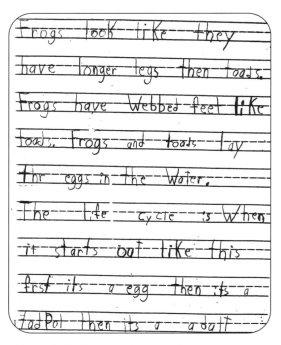

Figure 3.2. A grade-three student's report about frogs.

Teachers can encourage students to use new knowledge in a particular subject area in their writing. One year, when I was teaching a unit on the Middle Ages to a grade-four class, several students began writing stories during writers workshop depicting characters and situations from this time period. My experience tells me that once students are comfortable writing personally, they often write about topics and themes they are studying from the curriculum: bugs, settlers, heroes, animals, machines, families, dinosaurs, seasons, authors and illustrators, real and fictional characters, ghosts, frogs, and so on (see figure 3.2 for an example of a student who wrote about a science topic she was studying).

OTHER FORMS OF WRITING

Writers workshop is a place to introduce students to other forms of writing. Often, students will begin with expressive writing (although, be on the lookout for those students who consider expressive writing a form of torture). While they may try other forms of writing, such as journal writing or poetry, they need opportunities to use these forms in meaningful ways.

Present new forms of writing to students in mini-lessons during writers workshop. New forms of writing can be introduced with literature. A primary teacher might introduce letter writing by using *The Jolly Postman, or, Other People's Letters* by Janet and Allan Ahlberg. Or they might introduce poetry with Shel Silverstein's *Falling Up*. Students can be encouraged to try these new forms of writing during writers workshop if teachers and students share examples often and in meaningful ways. For example, a grade three teacher read aloud a journal entry she wrote while reading the story *Sarah Plain and Tall* by Patricia MacLachlan. In the journal, she pretends to be the main character, Sarah, a mail-order bride who moves west to meet her new family. Students can use journal entries as a form of writing in response to their own reading. In this way, students learn to use appropriate forms of writing to best express themselves and their ideas.

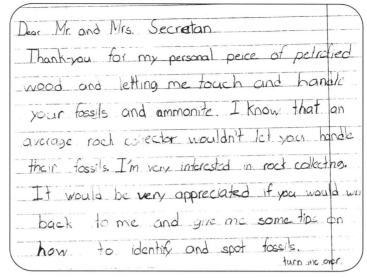

Figure 3.3. A letter written by a grade-three student thanking a guest speaker.

DOES IT WORK?

Students who take up their pencils and begin writing eagerly do so for two important reasons:

1. They have received the acknowledgment that their lives, no matter how simple they seem, are important to write about.

2. They have had an opportunity to tell their stories and get the kind of positive feedback needed in order to write and keep writing.

After a period of uninterrupted writing time, and this varies from class to class (I would give a grade-three class approximately forty-five minutes of writing time), ask the students if they would like to read their stories aloud. They may be a bit tentative at first, but with positive encouragement many volunteer to read their stories.

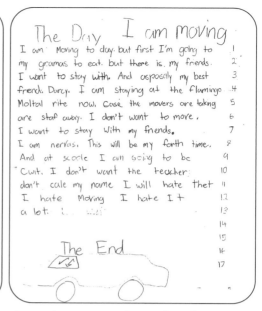

One Saturday Night

One saterday night me and my friend
Ryley desided to have a party. We
scruoched up a few bucks
frome auer parents then I
asked my sister candice if
she would drive us downtown.
she said yes becaus she loves
to cruse. We went down to
k.and t. and bote some junk food
then we whent to the movie
store. We got Encbino man.
We went back, home put on
the movie it was realy good
after that we playd a game.
It was abuet midnight my fric
had to go home.

The Day I am moving

I am Moving to day but first I'm going to   1
my gramas to eat. but there is my friends.   2
I want to stay with. And aspasaly my best   3
frendi. Darcy. I am staying at the flamingo   4
Moltal rite now. Case the movers are taking   5
are staf away. I don't want to move.   6
I want to stay with my friends.   7
I am nervas. This will be my forth time.   8
And at scoole I am going to be   9
Cwrt. I don't want the teacher   10
don't cale my name I will hate thet   11
I hate Moving I hate I t   12
a lot.   13
                                                  14
                                                  15
The End   16
                                                  17

Figure 3.4. These stories, written by grade-three students, demonstrate the quality of writing produced when students are allowed to choose their own topics and write about their own lives.

The two writing samples in figure 3.4 represent events in the students' lives that could only be written about by these particular students. One story is about a Saturday night in the life of an eight-year-old and the other is about an impending move to a new community. These writers demonstrate that no two writers are alike. Even when they write side by side in a classroom and have experienced similar instruction, they produce very different stories.

Drafting is one of the first steps in writing. These grade-three students used their writing class to get ideas down on paper, selected words necessary to express their stories, and attended to certain aspects of grammar, spelling, and punctuation. Most important, for these writers, composing (getting the ideas down) is separate from revising and editing (reviewing the piece to make changes and correcting mechanics of the piece). Again, Frank Smith (1982) and others have helped us to see the distinctions between these two processes and even how one can actually interfere with the other. Still, both processes are considered important to writing.

WHAT ABOUT KINDERGARTEN?

According to the Alberta Learning Document "Kindergarten Guide to Implementation," preschool students express themselves through drawing and later combine drawing and writing. However, the drawing often conveys most of the student's meaning. That being the case, the kindergarten teacher acknowledges and accepts drawing and writing as essential activities during writers workshop.

In writers workshop, tell stories to the students. Also, provide opportunities for them to tell their own stories, either to you or to one another. The story box titled "I Can Draw That" gives specific information for guiding writers workshop in a kindergarten class.

STORY BOX

I CAN DRAW THAT

Several years ago, I watched a video presentation of researcher Elizabeth Sulzby teaching a group of kindergarten students about writing. Her words and actions forever changed many of my practices in writing instruction. This is what she did.

Elizabeth sat on a chair surrounded by some twenty kindergarten students. The students had been told that their special guest would be teaching them about writing. To one side of Elizabeth was a blank easel and several markers. After chatting informally for a few minutes with the students, Elizabeth said to them, "I was wondering about the different ways that 'kindergartners' write." She made it clear that she knew kindergarten students had a variety of ways they could write, and she wanted them to talk about these ways.

To set the context, she reminded the students that there had been a recent circus visit to their community, and she used that as a starting point for their writing lesson. When she asked how many students had been to the circus, most students raised their hands. So she continued, "If you wanted to write that you had seen a clown at the circus, what is one way you could write it?" A student responded that she could draw a picture of a clown. With this in mind, Elizabeth quickly drew a rendition of a clown. She looked at it for a moment or two and then asked, "So, if I drew this picture and then read it like this, "Here is a clown I saw at the circus," you would understand what I had written?" "Oh, yes!" the students responded eagerly. "Well then, that's one way that kindergartners know how to write—by drawing!"

Elizabeth then asked, "Do you know another way that kindergartners write?" After a bit of hesitancy a boy answered that his little sister sometimes scribbled when she was writing something. Elizabeth answered, "Of course, sometimes kindergartners scribble like this when they are writing!" She drew several scribble lines across the page beside the clown. Then she added, "So, if I drew a picture and put some lines beside it like this and then read, 'Here is a clown I saw at the circus,' you would understand my writing?" Again the students nodded enthusiastically. She added, "Now, we know two ways that kindergartners write. Can you think of another way?" Several students offered, "We can write letters." Elizabeth looked and sounded very pleased, "You can? What letters can you write?" The students begin calling out letters for their guest to write. "*M*," said a boy near the back of the group. Their guest teacher recorded it. "I know how to make an *e*," added another student, and this was recorded, too. The process continued until several letters were recorded. Elizabeth asked, "Do we have enough letters for the sentence, 'Here is a clown I saw at the circus'"?

▶

The students all agreed except for one who said she thought they needed an *x* at the end and then they would be finished. The *x* was added. Elizabeth said, "Wow! Now we know three ways that kindergartners write. They draw pictures, they make scribble lines, and they write letters. Are there any other ways?"

A girl near the front of the group offered, "I know how to write some words." Several students nodded and shouted out their agreement. "You do! Which ones?" Elizabeth asked. The girl said she knew how to write the word *love*. Then she spelled it slowly so that it could be recorded on the chart paper. "L-o-v-e," she said carefully. She was followed by other students who spelled words they knew how to write. Many students offered their own names as words they could write. Elizabeth recorded and read every word that was offered. Then she looked over the page of writing that had been created, looked very impressed, and said, "Look at all the ways that you know how to write!" She reviewed each method of writing that they had suggested, acknowledging how much they already knew about writing. Together, she and the classroom teacher asked the students if they would like to go back to their tables and write something to share with their special guest. The students quickly took their places at the tables and were provided with paper and writing utensils. For the next forty-five minutes, the five-year-olds created stories, pictures, and writing. Some students worked independently, and others shared their ideas and work-in-progress with their friends. When the students finished, they had an opportunity to share the writing with either Elizabeth or the classroom teacher. They pointed to pictures or letters they had written, while explaining the page to their interested audience. Most students quickly returned to their seats to work on another page when finished.

This writing lesson is important because it acknowledges students' use of written language long before they begin school. Many researchers have documented children's preschool writing: they collected writing samples, discussed their drawings, writing, and letter attempts with them, and found that even young children are familiar with many aspects of written language. When children are able to write for their own purposes, as they do before entering school, they learn about many aspects of writing. Then at school, the teacher accepts and acknowledges the students' developing understanding of writing, while teaching and supporting new understandings.

Implementing a successful writers workshop in the primary classrooms depends on two main characteristics:

1. Organization
2. Routine

ORGANIZATION IN THE CLASSROOM

PHYSICAL ARRANGEMENT

Creating a writers workshop in the classroom requires attention to space, furniture, time/scheduling, and resource accessibility. It is important to create learning spaces that allow for independent, small-group, and large-group teaching and learning. This is because students first learn when interacting with others and then they learn on their own (Vygotsky, 1978). The examples in figure 3.5 demonstrate two physical arrangements that would enhance a writers workshop approach.

While it is advantageous to have students work at tables, it is easy to group desks together to create a table-like work area. The type of furniture the teacher has is far less important than what is done with it. For example, one of my teacher colleagues decided that her big desk occupied far too much room. She opted to move it out, store her own materials in a cupboard, and make room for a conferencing table to be used throughout the day.

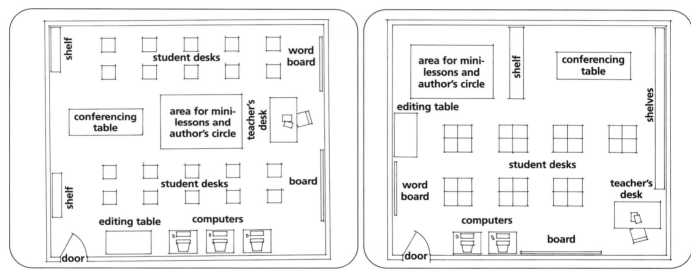

Figure 3.5. Two examples of classroom arrangement that facilitate a writers workshop approach.

TIMETABLES

How teachers approach their schedules is also an important consideration in the organization of the classroom. Yet, it can be overlooked as an essential part of maintaining a successful writers workshop.

I was recently involved in a school's evaluation and growth plan. Students from kindergarten to grade eight were asked to comment on positive aspects of their schooling experience and to offer suggestions for improving it. A common thread throughout the students' comments was the frustration they felt when classes ended abruptly and new ones began. These observations were shared with the teachers and administrators who agreed to decrease the number of short thirty-minute class periods in the timetable. Writers workshop is the kind of activity that benefits from longer uninterrupted time periods (forty-five minutes to one hour).

DAILY TIMETABLE FOR WRITERS WORKSHOP*

8:30–8:40 AM	• Take attendance • Calendar	
8:40–8:55 AM	• Mini-lesson: focus could be routines, writing technique, evaluation, message board, etc.	Students come to area of classroom for mini-lesson
8:55–9:00 AM	• Status-of-the-class survey	Teacher records on survey students' progress in the writing process
9:00–9:45 AM	• Uninterrupted writing time • Teacher conferences with individual and small groups of students	Teacher monitors whole class for first few minutes then begins conferencing with individuals & small groups. Teacher's aides & volunteers can provide mini-conferences.
9:45–10:00 AM	• Author's circle • Wrap-up comments	Students return to area of classroom for mini-lessons and author's circle

* Can be implemented 2 to 4 times per week.
* Times are approximate and should be adjusted to meet teacher and student needs.

Figure 3.6. Daily timetable for writers workshop.

MATERIALS

Accessibility to writing, drawing, and publishing materials promotes an inviting classroom environment. Supply paper of different sizes and colors, pens, pencils, felt pens (fat and thin), crayons, tape, glue, and stencils. Students who can find these materials on their own learn to move and work independently.

ROUTINES FOR WRITERS WORKSHOP

Once students have experienced the first day of writers workshop, they are ready for the many other aspects of working in this kind of environment. There are certain routines that enhance and simplify running a writers workshop. Some of the more common routines I have observed in primary classrooms include the following (see appendix G for reproducible master):

- **Mini-lessons**—short focused lessons most often directed by the teacher on some aspect of writing and/or writers workshop

- **Writing folders or booklets**—folders maintained by the students containing topics for writing, writing in progress, and published pieces

- **Quiet writing time**—classroom time devoted to students engaged in their writing

- **Conferencing (teacher-led or student-led)**—meetings between students or between the teacher and individual students to discuss aspects of a piece of writing

- **Author's circle**—a place where students can share writing in progress or published writing in a supportive environment

- **Editing table**—a table where students can take their writing to when they engage in the processes of revision and editing

- **Celebration or publication opportunities**—formal and informal opportunities for students to show and share their writing with an audience

- **Word wall**—a large chart or bulletin board that organizes new vocabulary for students as an aid to writing and spelling

- **Individual spelling books**—booklets containing high-frequency words for spelling as well as words requested and used by the student (maintained throughout the year by the student and the teacher)

- **Status-of-the-class checklist**—a form of recordkeeping used by the teacher to keep track of the writing done by students, processes engaged in, and problems encountered

- **Writing record (students)**—a form maintained by the student indicating the pieces written, including dates begun and completed

- **Writer's survey**—a list of questions posed orally (by the teacher) or on paper to find out about a student's perceptions of, and attitudes toward, writing

MINI-LESSONS

A mini-lesson is a lesson at the beginning of writers workshop lasting between five and fifteen minutes. It provides short, direct instruction on some aspect of writing and writers workshop. At the beginning of the year, use mini-lessons to tell stories and teach the routines and procedures of writers workshop: where to find paper and pencils for writing, where writing folders are stored, how to organize a writing folder, how to maintain a spelling dictionary and find other resource materials, when and how to edit, and how to share writing with others. When the procedures are in place and the routines are running smoothly (this can take up to two months), use mini-lessons for teaching writing techniques.

When working on writing techniques, focus on specific skills deemed important and necessary from curriculum documents, from your own experience, and from the students' writings. The following Story Box (page 40) provides an example of a mini-lesson from a grade-one classroom.

Jackson and Pillow (1999), discussing mini-lessons, write:

> Ideally, I use this block of time to present language strategies that grow directly from my students' needs. Realistically, there are occasions when I have to present specific skills mandated by state or district objectives…. Still, most of my skills lessons evolve from needs I observe in my classroom.

By beginning writers workshop with a mini-lesson, you focus the students' attention on writing and provide direct instruction on some aspect of writing. This time also sets the mood or tone for the period.

Students assemble on a carpeted area in the classroom in front of the teacher and an easel. The following writing sample is displayed:

i hav a fish i like my fish his name is tommy

Teacher: Today, we are going to practice being editors. An editor is someone who… (pauses)

First Student: …fixes someone else's writing.

Second Student: …and adds periods…

Third Student: Capitals, too!

Teacher: Good answers. Let's all be editors today, and see if we can help the author of this piece. What do you notice here?

Fourth Student: "I" needs a capital.

The teacher writes over the letter "i" so it is now capitalized. And so the mini-lesson continues. Students tell the teacher how to correct punctuation, capitalization, and spelling with this sample. The teacher finishes this way:

Teacher: When you finish your own writing, you can be your own editor. This means you read your writing aloud and look for ways to make it better, just like we did here.

WRITING FOLDERS

Teachers vary in their preferences for where students actually do their writing and how writing is stored. Some teachers prefer a coil-bound notebook that is divided into two or three sections. Others like one or both of the following:

- **Notebooks.** Have students divide a notebook into three sections: one for drafts, one for topic lists, and one for spelling words (figure 3.7). Teachers who use this type of format comment, "I know all the student's writing will be found in one place and cannot be lost or misplaced." They also say, "I teach my students to write on every other line of their notebooks so that their writing can be read easily and can be modified as well." One of the drawbacks of using a coil-bound notebook for writing is that published pieces of writing have to be stored someplace else, as the notebook is used only for prewriting, drafting, and editing. Sometimes, the format hampers revision because students may feel obliged to go with what they write on the page first.

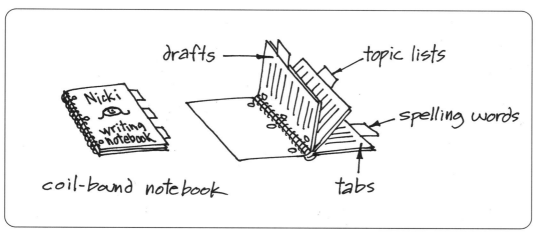

Figure 3.7. Writing notebooks.

- **Writing Folders.** One ingenious grade-one teacher has parent volunteers create a new writing folder for her young students at the beginning of each month. The folders are made from over-sized construction paper (see figure 3.8 for instructions). One side of the folder is used for prewriting activities and drafts of writing while copies of published pieces are stored in the other side. Because a new writing folder is made every month, it is less likely to rip or tear, and writing is rarely lost. Some teachers have students keep a list of topics for the month on the inside cover of the folder so it is easily accessible—a format that seems to work well.

  One drawback to the monthly writing folder is that students do not have access to a piece of writing from a previous month to work on at a later date. To counter this, folders can be made from material durable enough to last several months. Many commercially produced folders are durable enough to last.

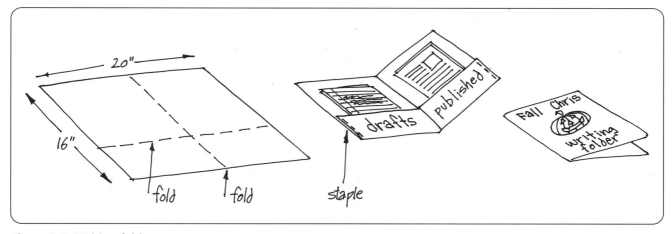

Figure 3.8. Writing folders.

Encourage students to use their folders or notebooks throughout the day to record interesting events that happen at school and to them personally. By doing this, they learn to look at the "everyday" things as an impetus for writing. When it comes time for writing, in either the notebook or the folder, they have a resource for ideas and topics.

QUIET WRITING TIME

At one time in our understanding of the writing process, it was believed (and to a certain extent, this way of thinking continues) that writers workshop would be a noisy place. Students would be discussing ideas for writing with one another, editing their work with others, sharing drafts and finished pieces in author's circle, and talking with the teacher and other interested adults about their writing.

While the importance of talk cannot be underestimated in young students' development as writers, there seems to be consensus among researchers and teachers that some time for quiet writing be encouraged and maintained. This time is referred to as "work time." It means offering students time to engage in uninterrupted writing time (Short, Harste, and Burke, 1996). Nancie Atwell (1997) phrases one of her rules for writers workshop this way, "When you confer with me, use as soft a voice as I use when I talk to you: whisper." It is important that students have support and encouragement while they are writing, but the focus should be on actual writing.

I asked a student to describe what he liked best about his teacher's response to his writing. The student responded, "It's how he says it. Kind of peaceful-like" (Bright, 1995). Many teachers, researchers, and writers agree that several things are important to writing: ownership, response, and an emphasis on students having access to uninterrupted blocks of time for writing.

CONFERENCING

My research of primary teachers' perceptions about writing instruction shows overwhelming agreement that conferencing is a great source of frustration. One teacher articulated feelings this way:

> *The whole idea of editing, conferencing, first drafts, second drafts, and how to do it effectively with one teacher and thirty students, especially in grade one, is very frustrating.*
>
> —Grade-one teacher

Why is conferencing so difficult in the primary grades? The answer to this question lies, in part, with the amount of time conferencing usually takes. Teachers know the importance of a response to students' writing and do not want to ignore this necessary aspect of the process. Therefore, it might be helpful to think of conferencing as occurring in one of four ways:

1. Teacher-student conferencing
2. Peer conferencing
3. Older buddy conferencing
4. Parent conferencing

QUESTIONS & COMMENTS FOR USE WITH YOUNG STUDENTS WHILE CONFERENCING

1. Before you begin, tell me about your piece.

2. Please read your piece to me.

3. What is your favorite sentence?

4. Who would you like to give this piece of writing to?

5. As you are reading, could you do some editing, too? Put in periods and upper case letters?

6. Is there anything you want to add to or change about this piece?

7. Where did you get the idea for this piece?

8. Do you have questions about this piece of writing?

Many other questions will emerge as the teacher and student look at a piece of writing together. With grade-one and grade-two students, the purpose of the conference is to develop a habit of revising. Do not be concerned if the student makes only minor changes.

Reproducible master in appendix H.

Figure 3.9. Conferencing with young students: sample questions and comments.

Teachers might also conference on particular elements of the writing process. As an example, work with students on three main types of conferences: prewriting, and revising, and editing (Jackson and Pillow, 1999). This method has the advantage of focusing students' attention on the "stage" of the writing process that they are in and helping them through any difficulties they are experiencing. However, at the primary level, it may be confusing to young students who just need you to focus on their writing without a lot of jargon getting in the way. Use both the student's writing and the sample teacher questions and comments (figure 3.9) to guide the conference. To be effective, the conference must focus on the student's writing.

Teacher-Student Conferencing

For improving writing, conferencing with individual students tends to be more helpful than whole group mini-lessons. Nancy Atwell (1997) advises teachers to "Get to every writer every day." Atwell (1997) also writes:

> My goal in writing workshop is to act as a good parent, with all the complexities that role entails... this does not mean that I've reverted to playing God and making all the writing decisions from behind my big desk. But it does mean I'm no longer willing to withhold suggestions and directions from my kids when I can help them solve a problem, do something they've never done before, produce stunning writing, and ultimately, become more independent of me.

The problem for many of us appears to be how to do this in the primary grades. Some researchers offer lists of possible conference questions, reasons for the importance of individual conferencing, and descriptions of types of conferences. But few offer the kind of detail needed to implement conferencing in the daily routine of writers workshop. To show one possible scenario that describes teacher-student conferencing see the Story Box, "Conferencing in Grade Three."

STORY BOX

CONFERENCING IN GRADE THREE

Tori Neely-White, a grade-three teacher at Jennie Emery Elementary School, begins writers workshop first thing in the morning by calling all her students together on the carpeted area in the classroom. First, she reviews the stages of the writing process by referring to large colorful charts on the walls. Then she reminds students that it is not possible for them all to be doing the same type of activity during writers workshop. She says, "You are all different writers. Some of you are drafting stories right now and others are editing. Some writers are brainstorming ideas for future stories, and some are publishing stories."

Tori uses a modified status-of-the-class survey to keep track of where students are with their writing and also to remind them of where they left off on the previous day. This is accomplished quickly by reading a class list aloud and having students respond by saying which stage they are working in. Tori gently reminds those students who don't remember what they were doing the previous day, to refer to the symbol she used on the class list.

> **D:** drafting
>
> **P:** prewriting (includes brainstorming and reading to develop ideas)
>
> **E1:** editing on her or his own
>
> **E2:** editing, and needs to meet the teacher at the conferencing table
>
> **C:** author's circle
>
> **P:** publishing work

Once the students know which type of activity they are to be working on, Tori asks them to go back to their desks where their writing folders have been distributed. Next, Tori acts like a traffic officer for a few minutes, ensuring students find their material and a place to work. Most students are seated at their desks with their folders open. Two or three students go directly to a round table at the side of the room labeled "Editor's Table." Six students stay on the carpeted area and arrange themselves in a semi-circle around a comfortable-looking chair in which one student seats herself to read her writing to the others. There are two computers in the classroom; two students occupy these and begin typing. Finally, three students stand at the back table waiting for Tori to return so they can have a teacher-student conference about their writing. Tori surveys her students, offering helpful comments like, "I can hardly wait to see where you are

▶

going with this story idea," and "Who will be sharing his or her writing first in author's circle?" Her comments seem to do two things:

1. They focus the student's attention on what he or she is doing.
2. They provide positive reinforcement to the student.

I watch as the students in this classroom are engaged in the activities associated with writers workshop. They do so with little direction for almost an hour. As they finish one activity (for instance, author's circle), they choose to go back to their desks and continue writing, join the Editor's Table for awhile, or sign up for the computer or for a conference with the teacher. Tori usually has two, three, and sometimes four students around her as she listens to them read their stories to her. She tells me that students in a small group can benefit from hearing the writing conferences she has with each of them. She is, however, careful not to let the group become too large. I notice she does not hold either a pen or a pencil during the conference. The student comes with his or her writing, a pencil, and an eraser. The student reads and Tori listens, offering a comment every once in awhile. "You read that phrase with such expression—like the character was really upset. What punctuation mark could you use to show another reader how to read that phrase?" The student then modifies his or her own writing. When I ask Tori about this, she says that she tries not to take the writing away from the student during the conference. She also says that if she notes a lot of errors in a student's writing she makes a note to work with that student during editing. For the most part, however, she focuses her attention on the content of the writing and on a few mechanical aspects of the student's work. She tries to take no more than four or five minutes with each student during the conference—these are added to anecdotal records stored in a recipe box on her desk.

Tori commented to me afterwards, "Sometimes a five-minute conference just isn't long enough. For students who need more time, I arrange a conference with me, an older buddy, or a parent at another time."

Peer Conferencing

Usually, Tori finds peer conferencing works best in one of two ways.

1. Peer conferencing occurs naturally for students who are working beside one another or who are friends. This happens throughout writers workshop when a student says to another, "Do you want to hear my story?" Tori doesn't discourage the natural sharing

that takes place while students are writing, but does tell the students to really listen to the other person and then talk about the story.

2. Students engage in peer conferencing through author's circle. Tori decides which five or six students will go to author's circle during each writers workshop. She makes sure that everyone has a chance to share writing on a regular basis in order to benefit from others' comments. Some students go to author's circle when they have finished a piece. For those who need some help and guidance in the middle of their writing, they go after just having started a piece.

   Tori also photocopies students' work so that everyone in author's circle can "see" what the writer is reading. She says this has made an enormous difference in the kinds of comments students offer one another about their writing. By having their own copy of the writing that is being shared, they are able to offer more specific observations and attend to those aspects of the writing that do not make sense. Students who are good editors even edit the copy and return it to the author after she or he has shared the work. Since Tori has implemented this strategy, author's circle runs more smoothly and requires her intervention less and less.

Older Buddy Conferencing

Over the past ten years, many classroom teachers have used "buddies" to help younger students learn to read and write. Generally, this means that one primary-grade teacher and one intermediate-grade teacher pair their students at various times throughout the year for literacy activities. Sometimes the buddies read to each other with material that the younger student is using, and sometimes they write to one another—much like pen pals.

Another use of this arrangement is the writing conference. The younger student takes his or her writing to the older buddy, who has been given some instruction about how to help the student as a writer. Together, they go through the writing to make it better. The older buddy can ask questions as a way to get the younger student to add or change aspects of the writing. Moreover, the older buddy can help the younger student with the mechanical aspects of writing (spelling, punctuation, and grammar). This type of activity should complement the teaching of writing that occurs in the classroom.

Parent Conferencing

The importance of the relationship between home and school in developing literacy cannot be overstated. Indeed, when it comes to literacy, the message from educational research has always been that families are important teachers (Bright, McMullin, and Platt, 1998). Parents ask important questions about their child's writing and want to know if their child is improving, if and when the teacher teaches specific skills, and how they can help at home.

In order to help parents play a role in the writing process through conferencing, it is helpful to go through a piece of writing with them and suggest the following:

- Students hold the pencil and eraser, making changes themselves
- Every single error need not be corrected

It is better if the student and the parent agree at the outset which errors will be examined. For example, they might agree that they will correct five spelling errors and all the capitalization and punctuation in the piece of writing. In this way, the student does not become frustrated at what may seem like a never-ending task, and the parent knows the piece of writing will benefit from some editing. Other suggestions for involving parents in writing instruction include holding parent nights, sending letters home, having parents help with homework, and conducting three-way conferences with parents, students, and teachers. Three-way conferencing can be an ideal time to show parents how their children edit and improve a piece of writing. While not all parents are able to do this type of conferencing, a three-way conference shows them what their children are learning at school.

AUTHOR'S CIRCLE

Author's circle is an invaluable part of the writers workshop. This is the place where young writers take a piece of writing, read it aloud to a small group of peers, and request feedback. Sometimes this occurs when a piece of writing is completed:

AUTHOR'S CIRCLE

The teacher checks the white board and notes that four students want to read their finished pieces of writing. The class sits on the carpeted area of the classroom, and one student sits in the author's chair with her writing. The teacher joins the class.

The student begins reading her story. She has written about the first day of school and mentions her teacher in the writing. On the first day of school, the student has written that her teacher taught the students a positive cheer to use, "To infinity and beyond!" When she reads that part of her story, it causes the other students to laugh. When she finishes, the author asks for comments.

Author: Does anyone have any comments?

First Student: I liked how you wrote about us.

Author: Thanks.

Second Student: Can you read that part again?

Author: Okay. (She rereads the sentence that caused her classmates to laugh.)

Teacher: Today you found out you could make others laugh with your writing. Do you have any plans for your next piece?

Author: Mmmmm. Maybe another story about school.

The students clap for their classmate, and she returns to a spot on the carpet. Another student takes his writing to the author's chair to read.

Figure 3.10. An author's circle excerpt taken from a grade-three classroom.

as mentioned above, author's circle is also the place where students share writing in progress and get ideas about what to do next. The development of a supportive environment, where students share their writing, is of utmost importance.

In my study of teachers' perceptions of writing instruction, conducting author's circles tended to be a great source of frustration for many of them. They cited some of the following problems: restlessness, inability to focus, and a repetition of comments (such as, "I liked your story"). Many teachers pointed out that while author's circle did seem to benefit the student who was reading his or her writing aloud to the others, the exercise soon appeared to become a waste of valuable classroom time.

Some researchers suggest writers read their pieces through more than once to help the listeners grasp the content of the story; others agree that teachers should photocopy or make an overhead copy of the story so that younger listeners can follow along more easily. The teacher helps students focus first on content and then on conventions. Figure 3.10 gives an excerpt from a grade-one classroom during author's circle.

EDITING TABLE

Many teachers, and some researchers, have lamented young students' inability or unwillingness to edit their work. This is what primary teachers say about editing with young students:

- Students who write well seem to get tired and have abrupt endings.
- They aren't interested in editing their work. Some would rather just start a new story.
- There is a tendency to let the teacher find what needs to be edited.
- Students want their rough copy to be the only copy they have to do.
- Students want to stick with what they first write.

These comments raise the following questions:

- Are we expecting too much from young writers?
- Can we change what we do as teachers in order to encourage young students to get involved in editing in a positive way?

One of the most telling anecdotes revealing a student's perception of editing was told by researcher Anne Haas Dyson (1989), who related her experience sitting in a classroom recording writing behaviors of young students. She watched a young girl write and write and write and was intrigued with the ease with which this student put pencil to paper. After some time, she observed the girl begin to erase some of what she had written. Suddenly alarmed that the girl was destroying what had taken so long to create, Dyson moved toward her and asked her what she was doing. The young girl explained, "Well, after we finish writing, our teacher likes us to go back and fix the mistakes but since I don't make mistakes, I put some in now." In other words, this young writer's perception is that she needs to purposely put some errors into her writing so that she has something to do during the editing stage of writing.

This anecdote tell us two things:

1. We need to find ways to discover what our students think about our instruction.

2. We need to help them learn to value editing and revising in writing.

STORY BOX

HOW NOT TO EDIT A PIECE OF WRITING

In my own experience as a grade-one classroom teacher, I faced some of the problems that prevent the editing process from being meaningful to our students. After my students finished composing a story, a list, a letter, or any form of writing that they would be sharing with someone else, I asked them to look at their work carefully and make the necessary corrections. To assist them, I often created forms or checklists for them to follow—either on their own or with a partner. To begin, I suggested they first read their work through and add or delete punctuation as needed. I surmised that this type of editing required the least amount of effort (searching for missing periods) and, therefore, would be easiest to do as a first step in the editing process. After punctuation came spelling. I asked my students to go through their pieces and underline all the words they thought were not spelled correctly. I expected that they would fix the ones they could do so easily and that I would do the others for them. Finally, I would ask them to think about changing words or phrases to make the story better. For instance, I would ask, "When you say water dripped from the tap, would you say the water was sparkling or smelly or murky?" The student would get the message that I wanted him or her to add a descriptive word to that particular sentence and would do so, sometimes obligingly and sometimes not.

Looking back, I know that I was going about editing in a somewhat backward manner. I only know that because I, too, am a writer—I now realize that it did not make sense to edit for the very small and minute details before looking at the bigger ideas. While I am speaking from personal experience, I think it is a mistake we, as teachers, often make with the very youngest writers. We give the impression to these young writers that editing is not worthwhile.

Find an opportunity to have students edit their work for a purpose that is important to them, as in the following example.

A grade-one teacher had students write their own ideas onto a page from a patterned story that had been read aloud. The students' pages were gathered together and stapled to produce what is often referred to as a "Class Composed Book." A few weeks later, just before parents were invited to the classroom for an evening visit, the students and their teacher decided to "publish" the book they had worked on and give it to the parents. Each student was given his or her own page to examine and to read aloud to a small group of peers. In so doing, and with the knowledge that there was purpose behind this activity of re-examining their writing, many of the students revised their pages for content rather than for conventions. When students reread their writing, they checked that what they wrote made sense to them as readers. They did this in anticipation of having an audience read their writing. This example demonstrates that young students are capable of revising for content and that this type of activity need not be reserved for later years.

What are some of the ways to get students involved in editing? One of the best suggestions is to set up an editing table somewhere in the classroom. It need not be a large area, but it should contain different-colored pens and pencils, a chart or checklist to help guide the students through the process, a tray to hold work in progress, and one or two hats or visors that students can wear to indicate they are now involved in a new activity related to writing. Just by having students physically move to another part of the classroom helps to signal to them that they are looking at their writing in a new way. Wearing a hat or visor is another way to physically change the environment and the writer so that the student knows he or she is now doing something different with a piece of writing.

It may be helpful to have students work with partners when editing so they can "talk through" what they are doing with someone else. Some teachers have students edit their own work, but others appoint four or five editors for the week to sit with their classmates and edit for them. Choose a method that complements the students and the way they work best.

EDITING STRATEGIES

- Set up an editing table in the classroom for students to go to when they have finished a draft of their stories.

- Have students wear an "editor's visor" when editing their own or others' work. This signals a new way of looking at a piece of writing.

- Each week nominate three or four students to be editors of students' writing.

Figure 3.11. Editing strategies.

CELEBRATION OR PUBLICATION OPPORTUNITIES

When students have opportunities to publish their writing in some way, it is an act of bringing the writing into the world for a particular reason. The four-year-old who created a "Keep Out" sign for her bedroom door had, in effect, published her writing (figure 3.12).

This is an example of *using* literacy, rather than *studying* it. Students celebrate their writing by caring about it and by bringing it into the real world. The preschooler who "reads" her writing to her mother on the way to the car is celebrating her writing. The grade-one boy who brings home a coil-bound copy of his story and reads it aloud to his family is also celebrating his writing. However, telling students they should care about a piece because it will be shared with parents, friends, or the principal is not recognizing why any author

Figure 3.12. The message is clear even if the spelling is not.

publishes his or her writing. In *Writing Instruction in the Intermediate Grades*, I describe the role an audience plays for publishing writing: "The audience can be as close as the writer him-or herself (the internal audience) or any individual or group outside the writer (the external audience), including groups that may be vague, distant, unseen, or unknown" (Bright, 1995).

For young students who are constructing their own knowledge of written language at the same time as they are producing it, sharing their writing with themselves and others is an act of publishing. Therefore, it is important that young students enjoy many opportunities to engage or "play" with writing. Sharing their writing is a natural part of the process of producing writing. Primary teachers need not be overly concerned that students go through the writing process in a lockstep manner where a published or good copy is the final product of every writing activity.

When students have many opportunities to use writing as they play, the teacher's role is to link their student play with their writing. In preschool and in kindergarten classes, this is achieved by including writing paper and tools in places like the playhouse, the building corner, the grocery store, and the post office. In this way, students learn to include writing in many different activities. While it is still important to have a readily accessible area like the writing table for students to engage primarily in writing, it is equally important to show the links between writing and other activities. These are the ways that young students celebrate their writing.

Another way that young students learn to celebrate their writing is through their involvement with writing for real purposes. When young students write lists for Santa Claus or notes to tell siblings to stay out of their rooms, they are celebrating their ability to communicate through writing. It is through the act of communicating that young students learn to value writing and understand that they have, in a sense, taken their work to publication. Publishing is the act of communicating in a real and meaningful way. This important concept should encourage teachers to view the writing process differently. Instead of thinking that each piece of writing must be corrected (and perhaps recopied in order to be published), the challenge is to accept the "act of communicating" as a form of publication for young students. This doesn't mean we can never ask students to add a period to what they have written or to correct the spelling of a friend's name they have used in their writing. But it does mean thinking about publishing in ways other than the strict sense.

WAYS TO PUBLISH STUDENT WRITING

- Make a book.

- Create a poster.

- Make a bulletin board display.

- Make an audio recording of students reading their own writing.

- Write and send a letter.

- Publish a school newspaper.

- Read stories to students in another class.

Figure 3.13. Ways to publish student writing.

WORD WALLS

During my classroom observations, I noticed that many teachers used word walls as an instructional strategy related to teaching writing. While this particular strategy is not necessarily new, it is becoming more recognized as a beneficial technique for promoting word recognition and spelling: two important aspects of writing development. There are differences in the use of word walls from classroom to classroom. Two formats for word walls are:

1. Use a large wall or bulletin board to display words in alphabetical order. This helps students to associate words with their beginning sounds and to locate words in a logical manner.

2. Choose approximately five new words each week to display and discuss. These could be high-frequency words found most often in primary reading material, such as *said, they,* and *the;* "doozers" (words that cause students problems in reading and writing) such as *to, two,* and *too;* or theme words that students are reading about. Figure 3.14 features two examples of word walls used in primary classrooms.

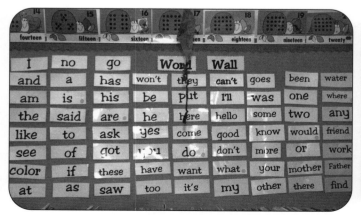
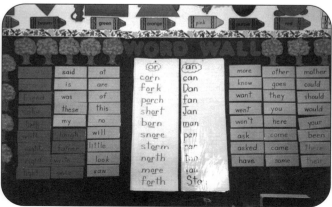

Figure 3.14. Two examples of word walls.

INDIVIDUAL SPELLING BOOKS

Many teachers create individual spelling books for their students. While this sounds like an overwhelming task, it can be made possible by following a few steps:

1. Provide a book or a photocopied booklet for each student.

2. Ensure each page is identified with a letter of the alphabet in alphabetical order so that students learn this method of organization for words.

3. Print twenty to thirty high-frequency words in the spelling book (printed by hand or photocopied). This practice allows you to keep track of some common words to be learned by all students.

4. Add new words each week, either by using a word wall and/or by students placing their own words in the spelling book.

The individual spelling book is an easy-to-use reference that students may access during writing. They may also take it home periodically for sight word practice.

STATUS-OF-THE-CLASS CHECKLIST

One method of recordkeeping during writing is called a "Status-of-the-Class" checklist (Atwell, 1997). At the beginning of each week, prepare a Status-of-the-Class chart (see the example in figure 3.15) and list each writer's name. At the beginning of a writing class, quickly check in with each writer (approximately three minutes) and enter, on the chart, what stage he or she is working on in the writing process—brainstorming for ideas, drafting a new piece, editing alone or with someone else, or sharing with others. After a week of brief recordkeeping, you can easily point to trouble spots that your students may be experiencing. This can be particularly helpful for young writers who, in the beginning, may get tired, stuck, bored, or frustrated with long periods of time devoted to writing.

Status-of-the-Class Checklist			Key D: Drafting R/E: Revising/Editing C: Conferencing PW: Prewriting		
	Date				
Name	March 21	March 23	March 29		
1. Tia	D	D	R/E		
2. Lance	D	D	D		
3. Jesse	R/E	C	P		
4. Pong	C	P	D		
5. Jennifer	C	C	P		
6. Ryan	P	PW	D		
7. Quin	P	PW	D		
8. Kodie	D	R/E	R/E		
9. Ruby	D	C	P		

Reproducible master in appendix I.

Figure 3.15. Sample status-of-the-class checklist.

It is also important to have verbal contact with each student about his or her writing on a daily basis. The status-of-the-class checklist allows this to happen since each student must be prepared to say what he/she is doing.

WRITING RECORD

A writing record is a form, maintained by students, showing the pieces they have written (figure 3.16). In the beginning weeks, the teacher and/or a teacher's aide might maintain this record. But later, the student should be able to do this. The record allows the teacher, the parents, and the student to note the number of pieces that have been written, how long a piece of writing takes, and the topics for writing the student is interested in.

Writing Record			
Student's Name			
Date Writing Begun	Title	Form	Date Completed
1.			
2.			
3.			
4.			
5.			
6.			

Figure 3.16. Writing record.

WRITER'S SURVEY

A writer's survey is an instrument used to gauge students' perceptions of writing. It can provide useful information about how students view writing, what they like or do not like about it, their writing habits, and their views of themselves as writers. With young children (kindergarten–grade one), it is beneficial to give the survey orally and one-to-one. Older students (those in grades two and three) could be given the writer's survey form to fill out on their own (figure 3.17).

SUMMARY

A writers workshop approach encourages students to write for real purposes, helps students develop fluency and independence in writing, and actively engages students in creating texts.

- Writers workshop routines are introduced one week at a time for the first month. After that, writers workshop becomes a more or less self-sufficient activity.

- Writers workshop is a place for story writing, but other forms of writing are also encouraged.

WRITER'S SURVEY

1. Do you like to write?_____

2. What do you like to write about?_____
   _____

3. Do you like to write first and then illustrate, or do you like to illustrate first and
   then write?_____

4. Is writing sometimes hard for you?_____

5. What makes it hard?_____
   _____

6. Is writing sometimes easy for you? _____

7. What makes it easy? _____
   _____

8. Which piece of writing is your best so far this year?_____
   _____

9. What makes it your best?_____
   _____

10. What advice do you have for someone who is having a hard time with writing?
    _____

11. Do you like writing "real" stories or made-up stories? Why? _____
    _____

12. Is there something that I do to help you with writing? What is it?_____
    _____

13. What do you need to learn to become an even better writer than you are now?_____
    _____

14. If you woke up tomorrow morning and everything was the same except for one thing—you
    could not write anymore—would it matter to you? _____
    _____

15. _____
    _____

Figure 3.17. Example of a writer's survey.

- The needs of kindergarten and preschool writers differ from the needs of writers in the primary grades, so lessons acknowledging scribbling/drawing, and emergent writing are needed.

- Attention to the physical set-up of the classroom is necessary: it facilitates mini-lessons, access to materials, and the establishing of routines.

- Teachers and students need routines for writing. Routines can be introduced early on in writers workshop, then at appropriate times throughout the year. A few of the necessary routines are mini-lessons, conferencing, author's circle, and status-of-the class checklists.

NOTES

CHAPTER 4

APPLYING

PROMISING WRITING ACTIVITIES

*It is a challenge to plan activities for students who are at many levels of
development, activities that will help each student achieve success and grow in
skills and self-confidence. Group writing followed by individual practice, writing
conferences, and sharing with classmates meets this challenge.*

— Picciotto, 2002

NOW WHAT?

Organizing a classroom as a writers workshop, encouraging students to write using self-selected topics, and involving them in reading aloud and editing their own writing (and that of others) are the bases for fostering young children's writing development. But is that all there is to it? Teachers have asked:

- What about the relationship between good children's literature and writing?

- When and how do I encourage students to try other forms of writing, such as report writing, journal writing, and poetry?

- Is it ever okay to have students write using an idea or a topic I provide for them during writers workshop?

Such questions show how teachers of young students often agonize over how to organize and plan instructional time to provide optimal learning. As Casbergue (1998) points out:

> On one hand, they (teachers) want children to write freely and
> discover on their own the meanings, forms, meaning-form links, and
> functions of writing. At the same time, they recognize that children's
> development might be aided by explicit instruction.

Researchers and teachers call for a "balance" between these two: discovery learning and explicit instruction. One way to achieve a balance is to develop a writers workshop approach to instruction, supplemented by writing activities that have been linked positively to children's development as literacy learners. In this way, teachers can offer balanced instruction by having students engage in meaningful writing while providing helpful intervention along the way. This chapter offers specific ideas for a writers workshop approach to teaching writing. First, help young students engage in writing and drawing activities that they themselves initiate and that often arise from their play. Then, over the course of a school year, add a variety of writing activities that support students' continued development as writers.

Defining "Writing Activity"

The term *writing activity* (Hiebert and Raphael, 1998) is used purposely. It has been used by researchers to refer to a type of learning that contributes in significant ways to a student's literacy development. Writing activities occur within three types of classroom contexts:

1. an event—literacy is used in the service of classroom community functions and other subjects

2. a lesson—teachers direct or guide students in acquiring a specific skill or strategy

3. an activity—students engage in reading and writing in ways that are meaningful for their own purposes and goals, either alone or with others

The activities that follow are compiled from several sources. They come from teachers (some of whom I have observed and others who shared their ideas through my survey), from researchers and literature on teaching writing, and from writers themselves.

Teachers can use these activities as described, or they can modify the activities for use in their own classrooms. Each activity includes a learner expectation, background information, a description of the activity, a next-step section, and finally, a "yes, but..." question regarding its usefulness for teachers and students.

WRITING ACTIVITY #1
"WHO ARE YOU?" STORIES

LEARNER EXPECTATION

An activity that focuses on having students write about themselves, their families, and other personal information helps students to develop an understanding that much writing comes from personal experiences. Since students are naturally curious about their teachers and want to know personal information about them (especially how old they are), this lesson builds on the idea of having teachers and young students share stories about themselves. Short, Harste, and Burke (1996) first introduced this type of writing activity in their book, *Creating Classrooms for Authors and Inquirers.*

BACKGROUND

The step after showing appreciation for your students as writers (see Story Box "I Can Draw That," pages 35–36), is to provide several lessons that allow them to show what they know about themselves and about writing. One of the best ways to do this is through a "Who Are You?" writing activity.

DESCRIPTION

- Begin by telling the students that they are going to interview you.

- Explain to students that they can ask any question they like, and you will answer them.

- Ask that they take notes of the answers on paper, so that they can remember what was said. Explain, "You can get to know me a little better, and then we'll do something so I can get to know you better, too."

- Students will raise their hands quickly and eagerly with questions: "Do you have any pets? What do you like to do in your spare time? What is your favorite food?" And of course, their favorite question, "How old are you?" (You don't have to answer that one.)

- After you answer each question, ask the student who posed it, "Do you have a way to write that down so you will remember my answer?"

- Eventually, every student has something written about you on a piece of paper.

- Next, the students can visit another classroom, papers in tow, and share what they learned about you with another group of students.

- A bulletin board can be created called, "Our Teacher."

- Display the students' pages around a photograph of you.

- Put the students' pages into a newsletter to be sent home: after students conduct the interview and record the information, have them read back what they wrote. Have an adult type the interview and publish it in a newsletter that students can take home.

1. Once the students have practiced their interviewing and recording skills with you, they can then interview other significant people in the school. The principal, the custodians, the librarian, the secretary, parent volunteers, and special guests can all be interviewed by individuals or small groups of students at various times throughout the year.

2. Have students interview one another or students from another classroom or school.

YES, BUT...

Should the teacher write the correct version beside the student's own work?

There is not one right answer to this question. However, there are various ways of thinking about this issue. Frank Smith (1982) makes a useful distinction between what he calls *transcription* and what he calls *composition*. Using the following chart, Smith outlines how these two processes are different, yet complementary.

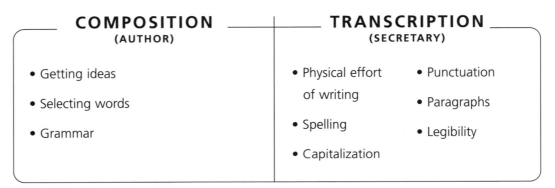

Figure 4.1. Composition and transcription processes.

Smith points out that, with many writers, these two processes (transcription and composition) are performed by a single person—the writer. Yet, with very young writers (three- to six-year-olds), it often is two people—the student and the teacher or parent—who collaborate to produce writing.

There are two ways to look at this type of collaboration: (1) the student and teacher facilitate each other's contribution, or (2) the student and teacher interfere with each other's contribution. Smith suggests that the act of writing, which includes composition and transcription, is so demanding that writers cannot attend to each of them fully at the same time. Younger writers are sometimes overwhelmed by the physical demands of writing, as well as the need to attend to so many processes at once. Therefore, on occasion, the teacher can act as a scribe. The teacher can write a version of a student's story, or write words alongside the student's writing, to assist in reading. The student writing and translation in figure 4.2 are an example of what one teacher has done.

It is also important to ask the student about his/her perception of a piece of writing. For instance, I suggested to my daughter, who was in grade three at the time, that I could help with spelling, capitalization, and punctuation on a rather lengthy story she had written in school. She seemed offended by my suggestion.

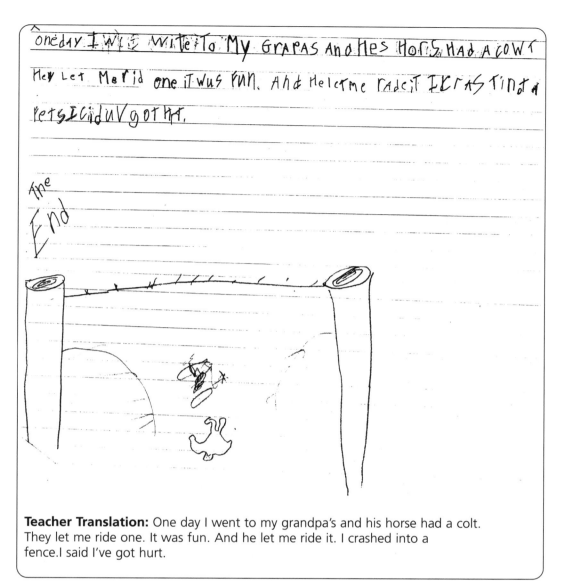

one day I wit write To my Grapas And Hes Hors Had A cowt Hey Let Me rid one iT wus fun. And He let me radeit I crAsTinota retsiciduV got hrt.

The End

Teacher Translation: One day I went to my grandpa's and his horse had a colt. They let me ride one. It was fun. And he let me ride it. I crashed into a fence.I said I've got hurt.

Figure 4.2. A student's writing sample with a teacher's translation.

In retrospect, I should have first commented on the content of her story and then asked what she thought she'd work on next. I would have gained a better understanding of her perception of my role. Did she view me as a facilitator or as an interference? Finding this out from students can help teachers decide how to work with individual students effectively. This can occur naturally during one-on-one and small group conferences with questions such as, "What are you working on? How can I help you? What part do you want help with?"

WRITING ACTIVITY #2
FAMILY STORIES AND PHOTOGRAPH STORIES

LEARNER EXPECTATION

The purpose of this activity is to continue to help young students look to their own experiences as fodder for writing. Build upon the writing begun in Activity #1, using family photos as catalysts for writing. In this way, students come to understand that they know more than anyone else about what is happening in the photo. It is up to them to tell others, through writing, what the photo depicts.

BACKGROUND

In an interview, Gordon Wells (1998) was asked to talk about his most important rules for classroom teachers in the area of emergent literacy. He responded, "One would be that reading and writing should serve a purpose and be meaningful to the reader and writer. That's the most important." One way to help students write in a meaningful way is to encourage them to write about their own experiences, to find delight in those experiences, and to share them with others.

DESCRIPTION

- Read *I Am Small* (Fitch, 1995) or *The Relatives Came* (Rylant, 1985) to introduce students to the idea of telling, and then writing, family stories.

- Use a similar procedure as outlined in Activity #1—have students talk to (interview) parents, grandparents, and other relatives; make notes using writing and drawing to remember what has been said.

- The students then spend several days sharing their stories orally with one another until the story has been told several times.

- The activity will likely yield several stories from each student to work on. Ask the students to make a list of their family stories and to decide which ones they want to write about.

- Some students will write several family stories, while others will write only one before turning to another form of writing for the next class.

- Each student takes at least one family story to author's circle (pages 47–48) and "publishes" one story in an appropriate way.

- Students may then decide to publish their favorite family stories in a newspaper that they can take home.

NEXT STEP

Provide each student with a short letter to take home to parents asking them to assist their child in finding a photo to write about. Include a request for parents to talk with their child about what is happening in the photo, where and when it was taken, and to provide any additional background information. Have students bring the photos to school, ready to tell others about them. Encourage questions to get at the "story" behind the picture. They may ask each other, "Where is this?" and "Who is with you in the photo?" When it's time to write, students will likely do so quickly and eagerly.

What about the students in my class who say they don't know any family stories or whose family stories might be too painful to write about?

This difficult question comes up often. It reminds me of Lisa Ede's (1995) observation:

> Writing engages students and teachers who have not only minds but also bodies and emotions, who bring to school not only their own experiences, interests, desires, and prejudices but also those of their families, neighbors, and community.

Such a statement raises uncomfortable questions for teachers of writing. Do we evade or confront the natural tendency of writing to expose what is there? I believe we should teach students to trust their stories. On one level this means acknowledging and accepting their stories as real and meaningful; on another level, it means facing some difficult and uncomfortable issues. Research into this area suggests that students in the elementary grades generally write about family support and fun holidays, accidental injuries and illness, relatives, learning new things, school, and friends. Others, researching students' writing in high-crime neighborhoods, say that people tell stories when something non-normative happens (Walton, Staley, and Fox, 1999). In so doing, these writers make these things more comprehensive. Walton et al (1999) write, "When we encourage students to bring their stories to the table, we are bringing them into the moral discourse of our culture."

Teacher Deb McDonald says, "Do not be afraid of what students will write. Writing can be a very therapeutic outlet for many students." Figure 4.3 shows two examples of students using writing to express worries and difficulties in their lives.

The teacher needs to thoughtfully respond to what the student has written about and, where possible, empathize with him or her. Sometimes, a phone call home can alert parents to issues and topics their children are writing about.

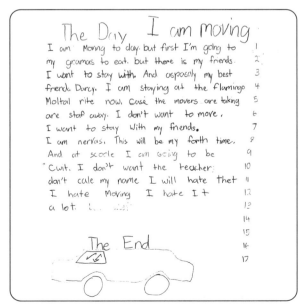

Figure 4.3. Students use writing as a way to express worries or difficulties in their lives.

WRITING ACTIVITY #3
WRITING FROM PLAY

LEARNER EXPECTATION

This activity allows students to extend their play with writing experiences. When writing is viewed as a natural part of the play process, students come to see its value even before they can form letters and words.

BACKGROUND

Play is an activity that comes naturally to most students. They often have ample opportunity to engage in play situations before they come to school, and they miss it when other activities take precedent. Ask grade-one students what they like most about school and, in all likelihood, the majority will respond, "Recess." Recess represents that special period when they have time for uninterrupted play. Many adults working with children suggest that young students continue to need time for play as a means to see the value of literacy in their lives (Casbergue, 1998).

DESCRIPTION

- Sociodramatic play is an important activity in classrooms for linking play and literacy.

- The teacher's role is to construct sufficient opportunities for play in the classroom.

- Ensure that students have easy access to writing materials such as different-sized paper, colored paper, and a variety of writing tools.

- Set up areas in the classroom where students can play during the day: house corner, building materials, dress-up, post office, fire hall, restaurant, etc.

- If writing materials are placed in several areas throughout the classroom where sociodramatic play occurs (and not just on the writing table), students are more likely to use them, and consequently, use writing for real purposes.

- Help students link literacy and play by being available to interject comments such as, "If you need to write a message while you're on the phone, here's some paper" or "Here are slips of paper to take orders in the restaurant."

- Model the importance of literacy by telling students when you are involved in a literacy activity, such as reading a note from home or writing a message to be taken to the school office.

NEXT STEP

Students who spend a lot of time playing in a particular area, such as in the dress-up corner, can be encouraged to write a story about their play.

STORY BOX

LITERACY AND PLAY

Recently, while observing two four-year-old students playing in the kitchen of a house-keeping corner of their preschool, I noted their telephone behavior. Each student was holding a telephone receiver and speaking into it. The first girl said, "Are you home?" The second responded, "Yes I am. Can you come over and play?" The answer was, "Just a minute. I'll ask my mom." She put down the receiver and called to no one in particular, "Can I go play with Zoey?" Then she put the phone to her ear and said, "Here I come." Just before she put down the receiver, one of the teachers looked over her shoulder at the two girls and suggested, "Why don't you leave a note for your mom to tell her when you will be back?" "Oh, good idea," the first girl responded quickly. She took a small notepad from underneath the telephone and scribbled several lines on it. Then she left to play with Zoey. In this way, the teacher was able to show the students how writing was part of their telephone play. While she didn't tell them they had to write out a message or check to see if it was done, she interjected that writing was an appropriate activity for their play.

Writing and play need to be paired frequently in primary classrooms. In the process of doing this, students use writing for real purposes and view writing as important, useful, and personally meaningful.

YES, BUT...

I have some students who would never choose to write if it was left up to them. What should I do with these students?

Involve students, who may not be predisposed to drawing and writing activities, in a mini-lesson. The mini-lesson, directed by the teacher, involves brainstorming the many different kinds of writing students might do in various areas throughout the room. They could be encouraged to draw road signs, maps, and signs for the buildings in a block or building area, or write phone messages, grocery lists, and room labels in the playhouse area. The teacher can also model this activity while students are actively participating in an activity.

While it is impossible, and undesirable, to make a student write, certain conditions can encourage and support writing. These include writing with a purpose, having ownership over the writing, and knowing the audience for one's writing.

STORY BOX

A TEACHABLE MOMENT

While I was teaching grade four, I was quite frustrated with my attempts to get a young boy, Jess, to write. His first journal entry read, "Hi, mi name is Jess." At first, I tried conferencing with him, but my attention seemed to make him feel even more uncomfortable. Next, I tried a group writing activity in which he and two other students worked together to create a story. Watching his group closely, I thought the others were "carrying the task" a bit too much, and I interrupted them with, "Please make sure you do some of the writing too, Jess." The other group members retorted quickly, "But he's giving us the ideas!" I went home that night and thought about what had happened. It seemed to me that Jess had ideas to write about, but the writing activities I proposed were not powerful enough to encourage him to write independently.

Lucky for me, in the next week while I was pondering my next response to him, Jess approached me and asked if our class could have a "Pet Show." In my mind, I was thinking of all the potential problems with his request, and then I realized this might be just the activity to get him writing. After all, he already had ownership of the idea. We met after school and brainstormed a to-do list. Jess recorded what needed to be done: a letter home to parents to tell them about the pet show, a letter to the principal requesting permission for the activity, posters for the classroom advertising the event, several letters to adults in the building requesting them to act as judges of the pet show, award certificates for everyone who participated, and thank-you notes to the judges and the principal.

I thought the task, and particularly the amount of writing it entailed, would prove too daunting for Jess. I was wrong! He attacked the project with vigor and commitment ensuring every last detail was attended to. In the end, Jess wrote daily for about a month. Unfortunately, when the pet show was over, he returned to his status of reluctant writer. But for one month in grade four, Jess found a topic, a purpose, and an audience for his writing. This is what we are trying to do for all students we teach. Some of what we do will be more successful, and some, less successful. However, if we are open to what our students tell us about themselves as writers, then we have a better chance of encouraging and supporting them as writers.

WRITING ACTIVITY #4
KNOW YOUR LETTERS

LEARNER EXPECTATION

This lesson, and others, help students appreciate that when they know the letters in their own names, they are participating in literacy activities. Often, a student learns to read and write his or her own name before recognizing other words. By focusing on letters and sounds in students' own names, teachers can gear lessons toward what is important to young students.

BACKGROUND

"The ability to spell and write one's name is an incredibly important first step... to know your letters!" (Cameron, 1998). This comment refers to a student's ability to recognize something of him- or herself in a set of letters called *a name*. When my daughter Erin was three, she began to recognize the importance of the upper case letter *E*. She now sees this letter everywhere—in an *Exit* sign, in a telephone booth, and even on the digital clock radio (in the form of the very square-looking, backwards number 3). Students become interested in letters and words when they realize those letters and words have something to do with them. Teachers can make use of this interest by gearing early writing lessons toward knowledge, recognition, and practice of students' own names.

DESCRIPTION

- Because a student learns his or her own name early in the literacy process, label a variety of objects and places in the classroom with students' names.

- It is important for a student to look around the classroom and see his or her name in at least ten different places—on the desk, by a locker, underneath the alphabet, on an attendance list or a job list, and so on.

- Use a sign-in page at school (see reproducible master in appendix L). One by one, have the students sign in.

Weekly Sign-in Sheet

Teacher's Model	Monday	Tuesday	Wednesday	Thursday	Friday
1. Erin					
2. Trey					
3. Breanna					

- Have name-writing samples from every student, and be aware which students recognize their own names and which are comfortable using writing implements.

- Over time, progress and growth can be easily seen.
- A game called, "Be a Mind Reader" (Stanovich, 1998) is useful as a phonics activity and a writing activity. This is how it is played:

1. Choose a topic or word, and give the students five clues with each clue becoming more and more specific.

2. The first clue might be, "I am thinking of someone's name that begins with the letter *D*." Have all their names displayed prominently in a pocket chart in alphabetical order.

3. Make the first clue somewhat vague, but have all students write down their guess before providing the next clue.

4. In this way, students are encouraged to "make discoveries" about letters, spelling, and words.

   Students discovered I was thinking of the name *Doug*. Another student offered, "His name starts just like Donald, and that was my first guess."

| Peter's Writing | Erin's Writing |

Figure 4.4. Samples of young students' writing. Note how often the letters of a student's own name appears.

NEXT STEP

Provide mailboxes for yourself and the students. In this way, students can mail letters, invitations, and send other messages to one another throughout the day.

Valentine's Day provides an opportunity for students to mail something to their classmates. Have students write only who the Valentine is from on the back of the card, and they can mail their messages to whomever they please.

YES, BUT...

Why can't I just teach students how to print their names neatly on a line and use proper letter formation from the beginning? Wouldn't this prevent bad writing habits?

Before coming to school, students have been scribbling, drawing, and writing for four to five years. In their creations, they have been making decisions about space (how much to use and in what way), intention (what it means), and experimentation (what it will look like). So, it is important to remember that young students already have learned a great deal about print conventions. They are not *tabula rasa* (blank slate) waiting to be filled with new knowledge. Rather, they take in new information and compare it with what they have already discovered on their own. For example, my four-year-old daughter, Erin, is left-handed and, more often than not, writes her name this way:

ח i ר Ⅎ

She watches her parents, her teachers, and her older sister print her name like this:

Erin

To date, she has said to me, "When I write my name I start here," and she points to the extreme right-hand side of the paper. "And when you write my name, you start here," and she points to the left-side of the paper. For now, I am content with the observations she offers about her own writing. As she develops as a reader, I will talk to her about directionality, using language that will make sense to her. Also, I will watch her work and, one day, when she experiments by writing her name the way I do, I'll say, "Tell me about how you wrote your name." By doing this, I leave the significant decisions about space, intention, and experimentation in writing up to Erin. But I do use samples of her writing as places for "teachable moments." I do this because one of the assumptions I make about written language learning is that language activities need to be controlled by the learner so that he/she generates and tests hypotheses about language. In this case, the hypothesis is that her name, *Erin*, is the same whether written left to right or right to left.

Teachers should certainly not ignore letter formation, spacing, or spelling in writing. However, when the teacher consistently makes these significant decisions and the student only has to copy, recreate, or fill in missing text, there is a misguided assumption that the student has learned the lesson. The student can only learn about spacing, letter formation, and spelling by making these decisions for him- or herself.

Teachers sometimes work with students who do not appear to be interested in attending to conventions such as capitalizing the pronoun "I" or words at the beginning of sentences. In such cases, teachers take a more directive approach in teaching these concepts. Some techniques they use include:

1. Finger spacing. Teachers have students place a finger after each word to indicate the size of the space between words and following punctuation.

2. Printing booklets. Teachers take time to help students with proper letter formation through daily practice.

3. Peer editors. Students check one another's writing for capitals and periods. They also underline words that need to be checked for spelling.

WRITING ACTIVITY #5
THE MESSAGE BOARD (SHARED WRITING)

LEARNER EXPECTATION

"Shared writing" sessions help model various aspects of writing and help teachers and students talk about writing in an informal, yet direct, manner. Such sessions provide an opportunity for teachers to address concerns or questions with all students. They also allow students to ask questions about writing.

BACKGROUND

Shared writing is another great technique to use in the primary classroom. The teacher writes in front of (or with) the students and engages in think-aloud talk. This strategy may be used for both whole-group and small-group instruction. It may take the form of writing "daily messages" on the board. One reason for this form's success in classrooms is that the writing conveys an important message related to the students' lives. For instance, the teacher writes, "Today we are having a guest speaker visit us from the museum. Do you know what he will be talking to us about?" This type of instruction is both responsive to the needs of the students, and spontaneous. Not surprisingly, researchers have characterized teachers as possessing exemplary characteristics when they "seize" opportunities for teachable moments (Morrow, Tracey, and Pressley, 1999).

DESCRIPTION

- Have the students volunteer ideas for writing, indicating that the form may vary. Sometimes they will write a letter, a poem, a message, or a journal entry about what they have been reading.

- As students compose aloud, record their words on a large board in front of the entire class.

- It is important to talk about not only *what* you are writing, but also about *how* you write the daily message.

  You may ask, "Who can help me spell this word?" "What kind of punctuation do we need at the end of this sentence?" "Whose name starts like this word?"

  It is possible to instruct students at a variety of levels of development with the above approach: those students who are not ready to respond will listen and observe, while other students will learn the names of letters and how to space words. Some students will learn about how to place apostrophes.

- Have the class read the message aloud.

NEXT STEP

You may continue with further language study by erasing some letters and having one or more students come up and fill in the blanks. The entire shared writing session can take as little as five minutes or as long as twenty minutes depending upon the length of the message, the interest of the students, and the type of teaching being provided.

After a session of shared writing, the class participates in writers workshop where they can practice their writing independently or sometimes in a group. Often, students use suggestions and ideas introduced on the message board to incorporate into their own writing.

YES, BUT...

How do I choose the specific concepts to work on during these sessions?

Only the classroom teacher can answer this question. It is the teacher who knows his or her students and their writing. No one else can know if students are stuck in one genre of writing, having trouble coming up with topics for writing, or need help conferencing with one another. As such, the content of mini-lessons must be responsive to student's writing.

However, it is possible and necessary to anticipate topics that will likely need to be addressed throughout the school year. Some of these may be:

- Beginning writing—helping young students recognize themselves as writers in all aspects of their lives.

- Launching writing—getting writers workshop started in the classroom.

- Choosing topics—identifying ideas to write about, from the ordinary to the extraordinary.

- Conferencing—helping students to confer alone and with peers in productive ways.

- Establishing procedures—developing and maintaining routines that support a writers workshop.

- Developing rehearsal and revision strategies—providing specific strategies to assist students with these activities.

- Discussing qualities of good writing—learning about author's techniques and styles that can improve a piece of writing.

- Reading literature—enjoying good stories and story excerpts together.

This list of topics is not meant to be exhaustive or interpreted as prescriptive. This topic list is simply a guide for teachers, who are the curriculum decision-makers in the classroom.

WRITING ACTIVITY #6
OPEN-ENDED WRITING ACTIVITIES

LEARNER EXPECTATION

Having open-ended writing activities ensures that all levels of writing development are accommodated in a single classroom. Open-ended writing activities allow some students to go beyond the confines of a particular writing activity if they wish. Other students can have a writing activity structured in a way that allows them success when they might otherwise have difficulty.

BACKGROUND

By bringing an open-ended aspect to all the writing activities students do, teachers have a better opportunity to meet students' needs as writers. One teacher-researcher points out, "My students are my curriculum. I want to nurture that uniqueness, not standardize my classroom so that the students become more and more alike, their aim to pass minimum competency tests" (Rief, 1989).

Writing Activities #1 and #2 are examples of open-ended writing activities. Writing "Who Are You?" stories and "Family" stories allow students to sample a variety of responses based upon their own experiences. Students can engage in these kinds of writing even if they do not know how to spell: they are using writing and drawing to express themselves. Each story is different, because each writer is different.

DESCRIPTION

- Examine the writing activity or assignment that students are working on, and ask yourself, "How can students demonstrate their individuality through this work?"

- Try to ensure that final written products are not identical.

- Encourage students to suggest ways that the writing activities could be changed to meet their own needs and interests.

- Provide students with choices of ideas, topics, and forms for their writing.

Encourage students to write on topics of interest to them through prewriting. One prewriting activity is brainstorming. Individually, with a partner, or in small groups, have students list on paper as many topics or ideas as they can write about. For many students, this is as much encouragement as they need to identify a topic for writing. For others, you might demonstrate how to find a topic that is personally relevant to them.

In such a demonstration, write a word, such as *blue*, in large letters on the board or on chart paper. With your class, brainstorm ideas that come to mind when thinking of this word, and create a mind map or word web. The board might look like this:

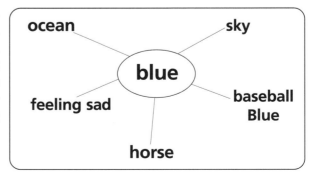

This activity shows how one word can be interpreted in many ways. Tell students that only the writer can decide which topic is interesting enough to write about. Also tell students that the writer chooses the form of writing to use. For example, one writer might create a poem about the word *blue*, focusing on feelings. Another writer might create a story about going to a Blue Jays game, and still another might write a factual piece about his horse, Blue. In this open-ended writing activity, students make decisions (with help when needed) about ideas, topics, and forms for their writing. More important, the writing they produce is unique and accurately demonstrates their own level of writing development.

NEXT STEP

If students are writing fantasy stories, show them and read to them a variety of fantasy-type books, such as fairy tales, ghost stories, pourquoi tales, science fiction, and others. Have students choose the type of fantasy story they want to write.

STORY BOX

POETRY AS AN OPEN-ENDED ACTIVITY

As a grade-one teacher, I can remember working very hard to make a beautiful poster (colored and laminated) entitled, "I Like Bugs." Bugs were described using adjectives such as *like, big, green, ugly, tiny, spotted,* and *fantastic.* After chanting the poem several times and pointing out the adjectives, I handed out pages of the copied-out poem with blanks for all the adjectives. I suggested to the students that they "make their own" poems about bugs by writing in the adjectives wherever they wanted to. In retrospect, the students were not making their own poems about bugs at all. They were simply recopying the words in a different order to create the illusion that they had created their own poems. At the time, this was pointed out to me in a rather unceremonious way, when one student simply refused to do the work and offered the honest explanation, "This is boring!" Now, it's very likely that some students in my class benefited from the structure provided. But I first needed to find out which students needed explicit structuring for writing and which students would take risks and discover things about writing for themselves. In my early years of teaching, I wish I had had the benefit of Marie Clay's (1993) words:

"Be careful not to establish a pattern where the student waits for the teacher to do the work. This is the point at which the student must learn that he must work at a difficulty, take some initiative, make some links."

Don't some students need writing frames and story starters to be successful? Is copying ever okay?

According to many researchers, students do rely on copying as a way to learn how to write. They copy print from the environment or from reading material to make a story. One teacher described her experience with copying in a grade-one classroom: She was giving a lesson to introduce journal writing to her young students. She showed the students their new journals (half the page was lined and the other half was blank). She asked them to do some writing so that she could write something back to them. She gave some examples and said, "You could tell me about something you like to do." Once the students had their new books, most began to write eagerly. However, a few students looked around at their classmates and appeared unsure about how to proceed. The teacher went over to each student individually and asked, "What would you like to write?" These particular students indicated that they would like to copy some printing from the board. The teacher encouraged them to copy the print, recognizing that some students needed more structure than others in writing activities. Over time, and as students' confidence builds, the teacher gradually helps them to rely less and less on copying.

Researchers suggest that some students rely on copying before they have developed an awareness of the connection between letters and sounds (Clay, 1975). A student in grade one, whom I recently observed, often copied the alphabet into her writing book. This girl apparently relied on the alphabet surrounding her classroom as a means to produce writing for her teacher. Her actions demonstrate an understanding that writing consists of letters; she also shows a somewhat less mature understanding of the correlation between letters and sounds. Through their copying behaviors, students demonstrate their level of understanding about writing.

However, as a teaching strategy, copying is not helpful to a young student's overall development as a writer. In his book, *The Meaning Makers*, Gordon Wells (1986) calls young students "re-inventors" of language. He refers to students' ability to learn how to speak their first language, not by mimicking or copying other speakers, but by trying

Figure 4.5. In this sample, a seven-year-old student uses writing to communicate his own message.

out their own combinations to get what they want. The same can be said for writing. The writing sample in figure 4.5 shows a student who is trying to use writing for his own purposes. Consequently, the writing may appear to be mistake-ridden to the adult eye. But upon closer examination, a message is being communicated, and the writer is showing us what he knows about letter-sound correspondence.

When young students copy perfectly what we have written for them to imitate, we are lulled into a false sense that these same students now understand the spelling, spacing, punctuation, and purpose of that writing. If story starters and copying are used in the classroom, the teacher can ask students if this is helpful to them as they learn to write. A seven-year-old who says, "The teacher's ideas are all right, but I have better ones to write about," does not need a story starter. But a student who is reluctant to begin writing without such assistance may be helped by these aides. Students, as always, help teachers make appropriate decisions about how to proceed with story starters and copying.

WRITING ACTIVITY #7
JOURNAL WRITING

LEARNER EXPECTATION

Journal writing continues to be an important aspect of any writing program. It provides a forum for daily writing to occur. It allows the students an opportunity to write without fear of being marked wrong, and it allows the teacher, the parents, and the student to see growth in writing development over the course of a school year. A journal is a place to write about topics, events, and thoughts that are important to the individuals, the teacher, and the social and cultural context of the classroom.

BACKGROUND

Many teachers use some form of journal writing in their classrooms as a way to get to know the students and to begin a dialogue with them about various topics. Some teachers carefully monitor what is written in a journal, providing topics, questions, and sentence starters. Others call the journals "Anything Books" to reinforce the idea that inside their covers students can write or do whatever they choose.

Whatever the approach, it is important to acknowledge that there are two possible reasons for engaging young students in journal writing:

1. To encourage an attitude that says, "I can write. I am a writer."

2. To help students figure out what they think and who they are.

Teachers who remind themselves that these are the underlying purposes of writing in a journal will likely be successful in encouraging students to value the journal writing they do and to enjoy the process.

DESCRIPTION

First Day

- On the first day of school, hand out journals and encourage students to write about something they like to do. Many will draw pictures of people and activities that are important to them.

- Students may complete the following sentence somewhere on their picture: "I like to _____." Model this activity for the students.

- The students and the teacher then share their work.

- Each student shows the picture and reads the words aloud.

- Students have written something that they can "read." This is a very powerful motivator to continue writing.

I like SPGSl.
I like spice girls.

I can xD MO.
I can jump on the trampoline

Figure 4.6. Samples of student writing taken from student journals on the first day of school.

Second Day

- On the second day of the school year, bring in something for students to examine, such as large and colorful sunflowers.

- Have students touch, smell, and take apart the sunflowers and describe what is special about them.

- While the students describe the sunflower, draw a picture of it on the board and label it as the students direct the work.

- Before they set out to draw their own sunflowers in their journals, have students brainstorm words to describe the sunflower (*yellow, huge, feathery*) and write these words on the board.

- Ask students, "Are you ready to draw a picture of a sunflower and write something about it?"

The Sunflower
Grows
grows.
T

Figure 4.7. A writing sample from a grade-one student's journal.

NEXT STEP

Throughout the next few months, continue journal writing on a daily basis. It is helpful to alternate between having the students write on suggested topics and having them brainstorm their own topics. On Mondays, they may be eager to write about their weekend activities and require little encouragement. School- and community-wide events can also be used as topics to write about.

Provide a mini-lesson at the beginning of the journal-writing session:

1. Model one way to go about the activity.

2. Reinforce a skill they have been working on.

3. Give additional ideas for those who need more challenge in their work.

YES, BUT...

How much time should I spend on journal writing when I also need to teach other forms of writing like letters, poetry, stories, and reports?

There are no straightforward answers to this question. Teachers are the major instructional decision-makers in the classroom, and they decide how much time to devote to writing and various writing activities. However, many teachers find it useful to think about their language arts programs in terms of three types of activities. These are:

- expository reading and writing—using informational texts
- literary reading and writing—using exemplary pieces of literature
- personal reading and writing—involving journals and responses

By attending to these three activities, teachers can ensure they are helping students develop fully as writers.

Over the course of a school year, plan units, themes, and activities that will engage students. The diagram shown in figure 4.8 (Johnson and Johnson, 1990) is helpful as a structure for teachers to use as they develop year plans in the area of writing.

WRITING ACTIVITY #8
WRITING FROM LITERATURE

LEARNER EXPECTATION

Having students use exemplary literature to support their writing acknowledges an important link among reading, writing, listening, viewing, speaking, and representing. Students may respond to a piece of literature. They may rewrite the story using their own ideas and experiences. They may illustrate favorite parts of the story or draw characters, settings, maps, or diagrams that represent what stands out for them in the story. The integration of reading and writing continues to show that reading influences, in a positive way, the writing students produce.

BACKGROUND

There is a body of literature that shows the strong and positive relationship between literature and students' writing in the primary grades. This relationship can be traced back to the work of Louise Rosenblatt (1978) who presents a view of reading as a transaction between a piece of literature and the reader. Eventually, it was discovered that students, through writing, could reshape the ideas from literature to generate new ideas. Indeed, many students began to "copy" the style, vocabulary, and themes from their favorite texts. I recently observed a grade-two class in which the students wrote and illustrated their own "Robert Munsch-style" stories. The stories featured young children as main characters often caught in hilarious circumstances. Many stories featured the often-used Munsch phrase, "You're driving me crazy!"

STORY BOX

STORY CIRCLES

Teachers call this activity "literature circles," "story circles," "reading response groups," or "reading reflection circles." I was fortunate to observe story circles in action while visiting Samantha Schultz's grade-three classroom in a small, rural town. The first thing I noticed when I entered the classroom was that the students were seated in various-sized groups. Some students were in groups as large as four, while most appeared to work in pairs. Each group had a sturdy, plastic basket that contained multiple copies (text sets) of a piece of literature and a colorful laminated page with a variety of suggestions for ways to respond to the literature selection. One pair of students was at the chalkboard working on a detailed drawing of a character in the book they had just read. I noticed Samantha listening to a student who was reading aloud. She had a clipboard on her lap and recorded short, anecdotal comments about the student's reading behaviors.

▶

I asked Samantha why she set up part of her language learning time as story circles. She told me that with story circles students were able to link reading and writing in ways that helped them learn about language through exemplary text sets. She found that students frequently used the literature as a model for their own writing. In addition, the students used writing to help them understand what they read.

This was evident when I sat with several small groups while they worked. For example, two grade-three girls sat together, each with a copy of *Charlotte's Web* by E. B. White. They had just finished reading a chapter and explained to me that they had taken turns reading each page aloud until the end of the chapter. They opened their "reader's response" logs and wrote a short summary of their reading. Shannon told me she was going to make a web showing what happened in the story. It is shown below:

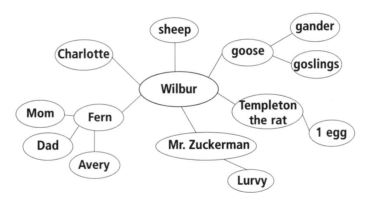

Her partner chose to summarize the chapter using a journal entry. This what she wrote:

Chapter 7

Wilbur just found out he's going to be killed when the weather turns cold. He's really really sad. He's crying and crying. Charlotte tells him that she will help him. Now Wilbur feels a bit better but I still feel sorry for Wilbur.

LISTENING & READING

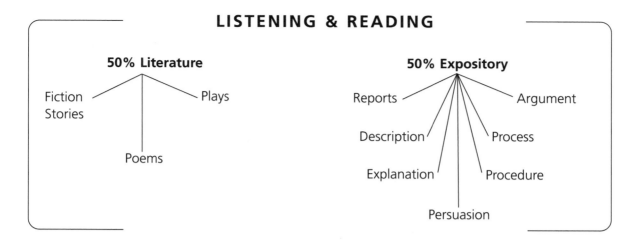

50% Literature

Fiction
Stories   Plays

Poems

50% Expository

Reports   Argument

Description   Process

Explanation   Procedure

Persuasion

WRITING

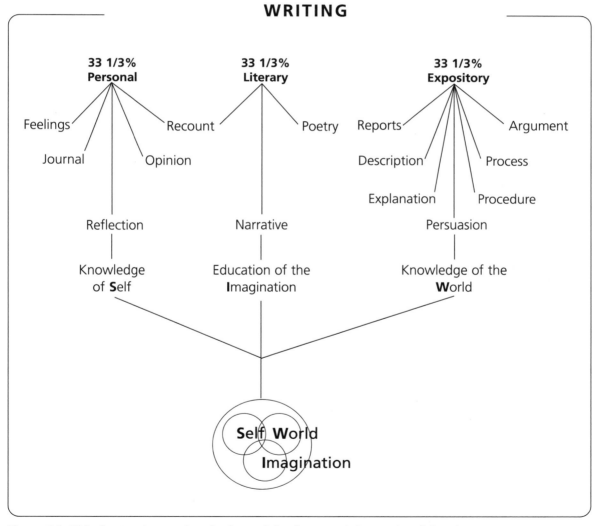

33 1/3%
Personal

Feelings   Recount

Journal   Opinion

Reflection

Knowledge
of **S**elf

33 1/3%
Literary

Poetry

Narrative

Education of the
Imagination

33 1/3%
Expository

Reports   Argument

Description   Process

Explanation   Procedure

Persuasion

Knowledge of the
World

Sel**f** Wor**l**d
Imagination

Figure 4.8. This chart assists teachers in determining how much instructional time is spent on listening, reading, and writing activities.

DESCRIPTION

- Make approximately thirty baskets of text sets, representing a variety of reading levels, genres (include picture books, novels, poetry, informational books, and short stories), and suggestions for responding.

- The number of books available limits the number of students in a group. Most baskets contain two to five copies of the books. Students form their own groups for reading and writing.

- Once the students make their selections, they sets goals for how long they will take to read the book. The group then decides how to proceed with the reading. Students might choose to

  1. Read silently, and talk about what happened.

  2. Take turns reading page by page or paragraph by paragraph.

  3. Listen to the story on tape, while following along in their books.

- Each student has a reader's response log, which may be a Duo-tang filled with paper. They may write on lined paper, but they may also use blank paper for maps, diagrams, webs, pictures, and charts.

- To begin, have students write the date, the title of the book they are reading, its author, and the date of publication. (By the time I visited this classroom in May, many students had read and responded to more than thirty books.)

- There are many ways of responding to literature during mini-lessons. However, the following suggestions are some you can model and discuss (remind students these are suggestions).

  - letters to the author and/or illustrator

  - summary of chapters

  - journal entry

  - sketch

  - chart, diagram, web, and/or map

  - Venn diagram

  - list of interesting vocabulary

  - summary of reasons for enjoying a particular book

- Students can also choose to do a larger project after reading a text. The students may:

  - make a diorama of a scene

  - role-play a situation in the book

  - create a mural

  - put on a puppet show

  - create a newspaper

  - make a game

- write a new ending to the story
- write a story using a similar theme, style, character, or setting

- At the end of the activity, call students together to discuss some of the things they have learned. The discussion may center around the themes of the books, the reading and writing they have done, or similarities to other books.

NEXT STEP

Students often try writing stories similar to those they are reading in their writers workshop. They may write:

- another version of a story they read
- a new ending to a story
- a new story with a familiar character
- a story copying the author's style

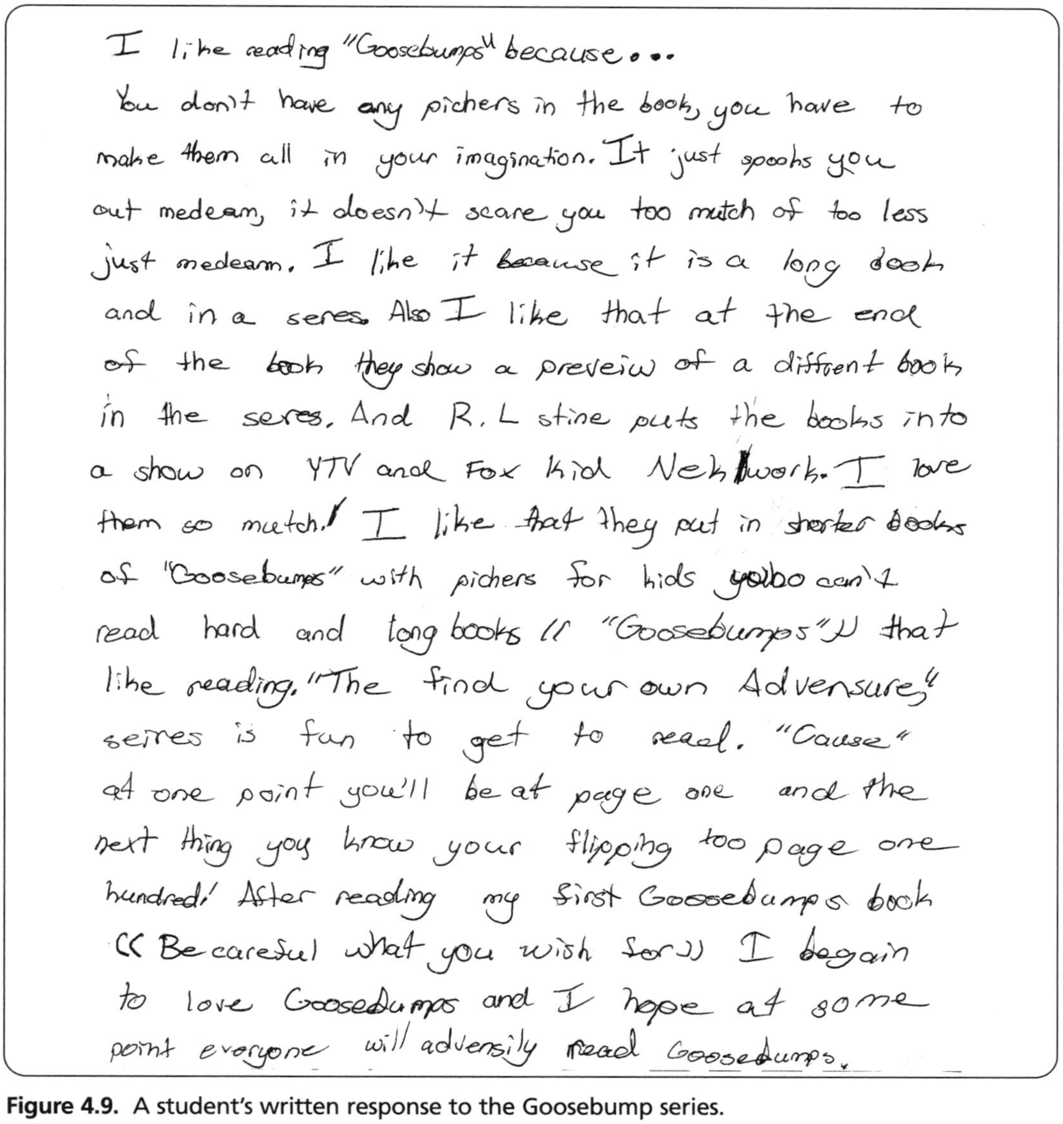

I like reading "Goosebumps" because...
You don't have any pichers in the book, you have to make them all in your imagination. It just spooks you out medeam, it doesn't scare you too much of too less just medeam. I like it because it is a long book and in a seres. Also I like that at the end of the book they show a preveiw of a diffrent book in the seres. And R.L stine puts the books into a show on YTV and Fox kid Network. I love them so mutch! I like that they put in sherter books of "Goosebumps" with pichers for kids yolbo can't read hard and long books // "Goosebumps" JJ that like reading. "The find your own Advensure" seires is fun to get to read. "Cause" at one point you'll be at page one and the next thing you know your flipping too page one hundred! After reading my first Goosebumps book CC Be careful what you wish for JJ I begain to love Goosebumps and I hope at some point everyone will advensily read Goosebumps.

Figure 4.9. A student's written response to the Goosebump series.

Story circles can be an ongoing activity. One group of students may take two days to read and respond to a text set, while other groups may take two weeks. Occasionally, the groups will have to finish up at the same time, so that group configurations can change. This will likely happen naturally much of the time.

YES, BUT...

I teach kindergarten and grade one together, and my students are not able to read books independently for an activity like literature circles. Isn't this too hard for younger students?

Even when students are not yet reading independently, literature circles can be modified in several ways so that five- to seven-year-olds can participate in this type of activity. Lisa McMullin and David Platt, grade-one and grade-two teachers, read aloud exemplary pieces of literature each day to their students. These books are then put into the classroom library for students to choose during readers and writers workshop. Students choose books by themselves or with a partner to read or browse through before drawing a picture as a response. They also use a Post-it Note to mark a favorite page in the book. The students then share their responses to literature by showing an excerpt from their book and by showing their written responses (a picture and/or writing).

It is also possible to organize literature circles for young students at times when parent volunteers or older reading buddies can come to the class and read aloud to small groups of students. Teachers often use this activity two or three times a week, rather than every day, to make time for other related language arts activities. See appendix M for a letter home to parents about volunteering with literature circles in the classroom.

WRITING ACTIVITY #9
HOME-SCHOOL WRITING ACTIVITIES

LEARNER EXPECTATION

Incorporating some form of writing that goes between the home and the school encourages students, parents, and other caregivers to use writing at home on a daily basis. Such activities help the teacher gain an appreciation for the range and the type of literary events that may occur in the home. There is also the opportunity to maintain valuable contact with parents and caregivers, which affects school learning.

BACKGROUND

It is important to develop a home and school connection in order to promote literacy skills. Bright, McMullin, and Platt (1998) write:

> Parents are a student's first and most important teachers. Among other important lessons, it is clear that home is where the foundations of literacy are laid. All homes are different but they share common characteristics that make them natural learning environments.

While families go about their everyday activities of eating, shopping, playing, relaxing, and getting ready for work and school, they use language and print. During the 1990s, we began to understand "family literacy" as a movement that acknowledged the literacy roles played by family members such as parents, grandparents, siblings, and friends. How best to develop partnerships between schools and parents generally is the focus of much research. How to do this specifically, to help develop students as writers, is the focus of the following school-initiated activity.

DESCRIPTION

- At the beginning of each week, encourage students to write a letter to you. The letter can be about an area of interest, a personal experience, a book, or a topic the student wants to know more about.

- Respond to student letters some time during the week.

- On Fridays, meet with the whole class to talk about the week's activities and events. Record students' responses on chart paper.

- Using some of these ideas, have students write in the Home and School Journal to his/her parents or guardians about the past week's events—what he/she has learned, any personal accomplishments, other relevant topics.

- Have students take their journals home for the weekend. The parents have an opportunity to read both the student's letter and your message. In this way, four messages are shared, two from the student, one from you, and one from home.

- All journal pages can be kept in a Duo-tang labeled, "Home and School Journal." By using a Duo-tang, new journal pages can be added easily, as can newsletters and calendars of upcoming events. In this way, there is only one "package" of information for students to take home.

STORY BOX

HOME AND SCHOOL JOURNALS

Janice Sheets, a school administrator, talks about a successful project she initiated across grades two to six called "Home and School Journals."

According to Janice, "The Home and School Journals… have succeeded in building better communication between the student, the parent, and the teacher… By sharing our stories with each other, we better understand each other" (Tompkins, Bright, Pollard, and Winsor, 2002). Interestingly, the Home and School Journal was first designed by this teacher in order to develop a regular communication system between the student, the parents, and the teacher. However, a second outcome was that it provided a document of unedited writing produced weekly by the student over a single year.

Naturally, the document clearly showed the student's growth as a writer over time.

NEXT STEP

The Home and School Journal is an important piece of the educational process. It establishes a three-way connection among students, parents, and teachers. It allows for key information to be available to the interested parties. It also assists in the development of the student's self-esteem by showing his or her accomplishments and comments about home and school.

HOME AND SCHOOL JOURNAL

Date: _____

1. Student's message to teacher	2. Teacher's response
3. Student's message to parent/guardian	4. Parent/guardian's response

N. xidneppa ni retsam elbicudorpeR

Figure 4.10. Home and School Journal: Developing communications between school and home.

YES, BUT...

What about students who don't return the journal on time? Isn't this a big commitment on the part of the teacher?

It will happen that students forget their journals at home. Take this into consideration when setting up such a project. Janice uses a form of positive reinforcement—she places a sticker on those pages that are returned on Monday or Tuesday. She also takes all week to respond to the student's letters, so even if a student does not return his/her journal until Friday, the process can still take place. Finally, because a new sheet is started each week, students do not need the entire Home and School Journal to participate in writing to the teacher. In September, when the routine is first introduced and the Home and School Journal is most often forgotten, a phone call home (by either the student or the teacher) helps to indicate its importance at school.

When the Home and School Journal is started in September, explain the process to parents during a "Back-to-School Night" and in a letter. It is important to make contact with parents to explain the nature of the project before the journal goes home for the first time. It is also important to encourage parents to focus on the message, and to point out that friendly letters are not edited by the person receiving them, but enjoyed for what they say.

Janice acknowledges that maintaining a Home and School Journal on a weekly basis is a big commitment (and confesses there are weeks when the journals are not used). However, at the end of the year, both the students and their parents enjoy looking through the journal to see all the accomplishments and growth in writing. Janice says, "The rewards and relationships built are well worth it!"

WRITING ACTIVITY #10
WRITING ACROSS THE CURRICULUM

LEARNER EXPECTATION

More and more, one hears about the "integrated curriculum." An integrated curriculum focuses less on the knowledge and skills of a particular discipline (such as language, mathematics, art, and physical education) and more on knowledge systems across subject areas. Students must engage in writing as a way to explore and share meaning across the curriculum.

BACKGROUND

According to many researchers, there is a natural link between writing and thinking. Underlying this idea is the assumption that the act of writing leads to better understanding. However, it is important to note that the type of writing we engage students in matters.

Informal writing experiences have been compared to engaging in a written conversation with oneself or with an interested peer or adult. There are seven purposes for using informal types of writing:

1. Writing to get ready to learn.

2. Writing to explore thinking.

3. Writing to make learning personal.

4. Writing to struggle with difficult learning.

5. Writing to think independently.

6. Writing to wonder.

7. Writing to engage the imagination.

In *Language Across the Curriculum: The Primary Handbook* (1992), the authors suggest writing should be used to help students work through the process of learning. This is done by providing support and encouraging students to reflect upon their learning.

DESCRIPTION

Writing activities that provide a greater depth of understanding across the curriculum include the following:

- K-W-L chart

- Compare and contrast chart (Venn diagram)

- Freewriting

- Report writing

- Concept map (clustering)

- Learning logs

- Note-taking

STORY BOX

WRITING AND LEARNING

My ten-year old daughter was sharing her report card with us. When her father and I complimented her on achieving first-rate grades in her subjects, she pointed to her social studies mark and replied, "Even though I got an *A* in social studies, I didn't really learn the stuff." It turned out the "stuff" she was referring to included the study of early Canadian explorers. When I asked her how she was able to achieve an *A* on her report card without learning anything, her response was quite logical. Learning in social studies involved reading the textbook, filling in the blanks on a worksheet, and memorizing the same material to regurgitate on an exam. When the exam was over, the information was forgotten. What I found interesting about this conversation with my daughter was her ability to distinguish between writing used for short-term recall and writing used for meaningful learning.

K-W-L Chart

The K-W-L (Ogle, 1986) is a strategy used to introduce a new unit of study. Using the chart format in figure 4.11, have students:

- brainstorm their Knowledge about a topic (such as "ocean life")
- discuss what they Want to know about the topic
- indicate what they have Learned.

At the primary level, a K-W-L chart can be made using large chart paper and displayed on a bulletin board throughout the unit. Students add information to the chart as they learn new information. The chart becomes a way for students to visualize their learning process.

K-W-L STRATEGY

Topic: _____

What do I know?	What do I want to know?	What have I learned?

Reproducible master in appendix O.

Figure 4.11. K-W-L chart.

COMPARE AND CONTRAST CHART (VENN DIAGRAM)

A compare and contrast chart is used to categorize information into two main areas:

1. The differences between the two categories.

2. The similarities between the two categories.

Teachers often use two large Hula-Hoops to demonstrate this approach to young students. The Hula-Hoops are placed on the floor side by side. As the students study a particular topic, they find pictures (or cards produced by the teacher) and sort them into two differing groups, as indicated below. The Hula-Hoops can then be linked together to show that some items can be categorized in two ways.

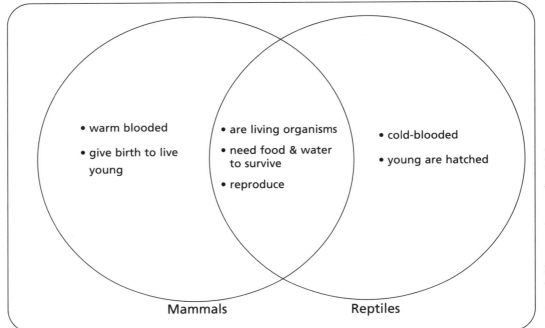

Figure 4.12. Compare and contrast chart (Venn diagram).

In the beginning, record the information on chart paper, then later encourage students to develop and write out their own compare and contrast charts. Grade-one students can be successful creating and filling in compare and contrast charts when they are oversized to accommodate large and, sometimes, less-controlled printing.

FREEWRITING

Freewriting is an informal writing strategy that can be used in many different contexts to improve writing fluency. Freewriting may be used for expressive writing (as in a diary or a journal), or it may be used, for example, to respond to a film about penguins. Students need to be encouraged to write down their thoughts, ideas, and feelings in an uninterrupted period of time, without any constraints.

One idea is to tell students that they have five minutes to "freewrite" about a particular topic, concept, event, or phrase. You may choose the topic or ask students to come up with their own. Their writing may then be used as a basis for a class discussion or as the first step in writing a report, or it may become part of the writing portfolio to be examined at a later date. Figure 4.13 shows an example of a grade-one student's freewrite in response to a school event.

WRITE FROM THE START

REPORT WRITING

Should primary students engage in report writing? Many teachers believe that report writing should be part of a language arts program from the time young students begin to write. Research also demonstrates that students in the elementary grades can successfully search for answers to questions that interest them and report on these, both collaboratively and individually.

Students learn important reading and writing skills through report writing. For some students, writing a fictional story is not as meaningful as writing nonfiction, and this preference for one genre over another can also be seen in their reading. So, it makes sense to provide opportunities for writing in a variety of forms.

Younger students can dictate their reports to the teacher or write collaboratively in small groups.

Figure 4.13. A "freewrite" by a grade-one student.

STORY BOX

REPORT WRITING IN GRADE THREE

To illustrate report writing with young students, here is a class activity designed and implemented by a grade-three teacher. The students were studying swamps as part of the science curriculum. After reading several fiction and nonfiction stories about frogs and viewing videotapes related to the topic of frogs, the teacher asked the students to brainstorm what they had learned. This was a whole-class activity, and answers were recorded on large chart paper by the teacher. Next, the teacher handed out large sheets of paper containing possible topics for students to use to categorize their information (see appendix R).

The students were then asked to use the information they had recorded on their charts to write a report showing what they knew about frogs. Each student wrote a first draft and read this to a peer, who indicated (1) what he or she liked about the report, and (2) what could be changed. Most suggested changes were about spelling, punctuation, and capitalization. The students then each produced a final copy and illustrated it. These were then shared with other primary-aged students in the school.

▶

Crystal's Chart on Frogs

looks [frogs] cr ls tal		have Webbed feet	babies
frogs look Like thay are Longer Butes than toads. frogs Look Like thay are Big		thay hav eyes on thr hed thay are green	thay lay thr eggs in the water.

lives	eats	enemies	can do
frogs live In water and on land.	insects Shells	Turtles fish. snakes bird Owl	frogs. can Hibernate In the winter. frogs can swim. frogs can Jup.

Crystal's Report on Frogs

rogs and toads live in the water and on land. Frogs can Jump and Hibernate In The winter. frogs and toads enemies are turtles, fish, snakes, birds, owl. frogs and toads eat snells.

CONCEPT MAP (CLUSTERING)

A concept map is a diagram where the words generated are circled and linked to a nucleus (main) word. The result is a web-like diagram, rather than a list. Teachers generally direct an activity like this in order to get students thinking about a topic or an idea.

- The topic is chosen and written in a circle in the center of a page.
- Rays are formed linking the circle to other ideas.
- Rays are added as necessary to provide new information, details, and sub-topics.

In practice, however, creating a concept map is usually a "messy" endeavor (figure 4.14).

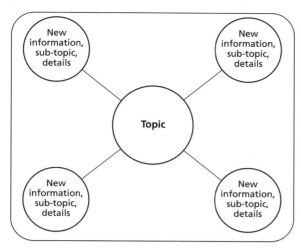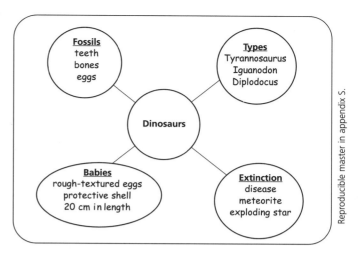

Reproducible master in appendix S.

Figure 4.14. Example of a concept map.

LEARNING LOGS

Learning logs can be used in a variety of subjects. They provide opportunities for students to reflect on and extend their learning. Students can maintain a general learning log for all subjects or a specific learning log for mathematics, science, art, social studies, or drama. Teachers may have a learning log scribbler, Duo-tang, scrapbook, or any other book for students to maintain. One learning log can be used for a variety of subjects in the primary grades.

Encourage students to respond to a new concept, idea, or reading by writing, drawing, asking questions, and making statements. Learning logs can also be a catalyst for students to talk to one another and to the teacher about their perspectives and questions. The following observation about the importance of self-reflection to learning is helpful to remember: "Learners (also) need time to reflect on their learning experiences in school and the processes they have used in that learning" (Short, Harste, and Burke, 1996).

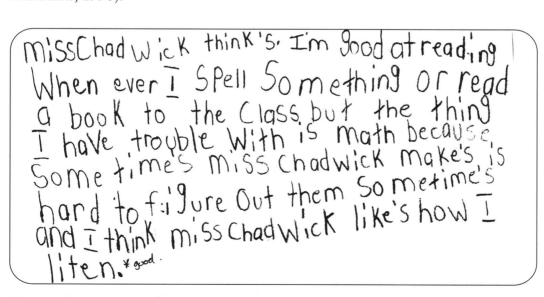

Figure 4.15. A student's reflection on her learning.

Furthermore, teachers can review a student's learning log prior to reporting progress to parents. Examine and discuss entries in order to reflect upon what the student has learned and what new learning goals need to be set.

NOTE-TAKING

Note-taking, as a strategy for across-curriculum learning, actually begins in the primary grades. Note-taking is a strategy that permits an "efficient stance" toward information. That is, reading, writing, listening or speaking, and viewing skills are used to comprehend and understand information and "to carry away" that same information.

Young students can be taught note-taking as a way to remember something they have heard, observed, or learned. For example, while watching a videotape on dinosaurs, pause the tape in order to model writing down information you want to remember. Model invented spelling and use pictures for some ideas. The following list is an example of note-taking:

- Dinosaurs
- T-rex
- Short arms
- Teeth 18cm long
- Meat eater
- Sharp teeth

In kindergarten and grade one, model note-taking, but in grades two and three, have students do this activity on their own. They can take notes while watching a videotape, interviewing a special person, listening to a guest speaker, or going on a field trip. The important aspect of note-taking is that students see the value of recording and remembering information for specific purposes. Those purposes may vary from classroom to classroom but should focus on helping students understand information.

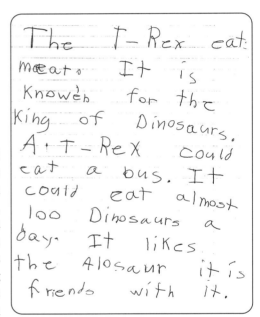

Figure 4.16. A grade-two student makes notes from a book about dinosaurs.

YES, BUT...

Should primary-aged students be writing research reports? Isn't this better left to teachers in grades four to six?

It may seem, at first, that report writing is too complex for young students. However, consider that many students who are uninterested in reading and writing fiction can be "hooked in" to reading and writing informational texts. You can meet individual student's interest in dinosaurs, BMX racing, or the solar system by providing informational reading and writing activities that would not be possible when students are all required to read and write the same thing. Students can learn the same language skills whether they are writing a personal journal entry or a new fact they have discovered about dolphins.

SUMMARY

- Writing activities are occasions for students to engage in reading and writing (either alone or with others) that are meaningful for their own purposes and goals.

- The ten writing activities found in this chapter represent the most promising practices for primary students as articulated by teachers, researchers, and writers.

- Each writing activity can be modified to meet the needs of students, the teacher, and the curriculum.

- Questions posed about each writing activity help teachers clarify their own thinking about the usefulness and applicability of the activity. These are not recipes for good writing, only possible starting points.

- The focus for writing should always be on connecting students' writing with the topics, experiences, and issues in their lives.

NOTES

CHAPTER 5

VALUING

RESPONDING TO AND EVALUATING
STUDENTS' WRITING

*In order to develop as better writers, students need opportunities to step
back from their writing and reflect on the content and processes involved.
Then they can make a judgement about their own performance as
individual writers and learners.* — Hill, 1990

This chapter focuses on ways to respond to and evaluate students' writing. Topics
addressed include student self-assessment, assessing writing competency, and
creating a student writing profile. In addition, suggestions are provided to help
teachers examine resources and strategies to get organized and enlist the help of
parents.

WHAT ARE ASSESSMENT AND EVALUATION?

Teachers form the primary audience for students' writing and, as such, are called
upon to judge how well a student is doing. Is the student developing in similar ways
to his or her peers? Is the student meeting provincial/state guidelines for progress?
Is the student above or below these guidelines? In thinking about valuing students'
writing, two terms are used:

1. Assessment

Assessment is the gathering and reviewing of documentation in order to make
decisions about how to help students develop as writers. Documentation can include
student self-assessments, writing samples, interviews with students, teachers' anecdotal records, checklists, and observations.

2. Evaluation

Evaluation is the judgment made about the quality of a student's writing in
relation to provincial/state curriculum standards, rubrics, or other exemplary work.

In the primary grades, a teacher spends a great deal of time gathering
documentation and assessing student writing. The teacher evaluates student writing
three or four times a year in order to tell parents about their child's progress. However,
teachers are not the only audience for students' writing: students themselves are an
important audience. To illustrate, some students will tell their teacher that they do
not want to read a piece aloud as it is only for them. Classmates provide another
audience, as do good friends and family members.

Assessing and Evaluating the Program

When engaged in evaluating writing, ask yourself the following interrelated questions:

- Are my students learning to write?

- Do I have sufficient resources to meet my students' needs?

- Do I use teaching activities that work?

- Is my organization of writers workshop conducive to the writing developmental levels of my students?

These questions, while focusing on the students' development as writers, ask you to consider your important role in setting up activities for helping students learn to write. These questions need to be asked several times throughout the school year in order to establish and maintain a writing program that works for you and your students.

Responding to Student Writing

According to Peter Elbow (2000), most teachers give "impoverished" responses to students' writing. He outlines three types of responses that we can give to our students:

1. Evaluative responses

2. Non-evaluative responses

3. No response, merely sharing

1. Evaluative responses are those that teachers are most familiar with. We use evaluative responses when we mark or grade a student's writing using a set of criteria or our own experience to judge work.

2. Non-evaluative responses offer comments or questions about a piece of writing without talking about either its quality or its value. With non-evaluative responses, teachers ask, "What is this story about?" or "How do you want the reader to feel when he or she reads this piece?"

3. No response occurs when students are asked to read their writing in front of an audience for the sole purpose of reading the piece aloud. The audience claps and the writer thanks the audience. Elbow believes that this may be one of the most helpful kinds of responses writers can receive, because students hear for themselves how their writing sounds. He notes that students may stop their reading to explain a part of the writing when they themselves note that something may be missing or may be confusing to the audience.

The above responses are helpful in supporting student writing. It is important to note that Elbow does not consider any one of these responses to be superior, but argues for using all of them equally with students.

TYPES OF DOCUMENTATION IN WRITING

There are many ways to gather information to assess and evaluate students' writing. Some of these involve looking at students' written products. Others involve watching and documenting students' writing processes as well as using students' own insights about themselves as writers. The following ways to gather information about student writing will be presented:

- Writing samples
- Anecdotal observations
- Students' self-assessments
- Student interviews
- Writer's profile

WRITING SAMPLES

Students' own writing can be one of the most powerful methods of assessing and evaluating how they are developing as writers. This is especially true if students have opportunities to write stories that are wholly their own. Writing that is done using story starters or fill-in-the-blank pages do not often contain enough of the student's own writing to be a useful indicator of writing ability. A student's own writing, however, can be helpful when deciding how best to help a young writer progress.

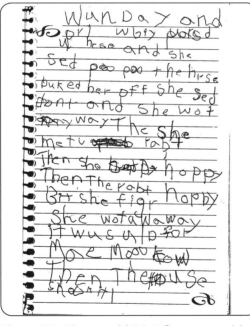

One day a
girl walked passed
a horse and she
said poo poo. The horse
bucked her off. She said
don't and she went
away. Then she
met a rabbit.
Then she said hoppy hoppy.
Then the rabbit
bit her finger.
She walked away.
It was a for
Mary Moo Cow.
Then the house
shook… (interrupted)

Figure 5.1. Six-year-old Erin's first story writing sample and translation.

The wrting sample in figure 5.1 shows Erin using both standard spelling—*day, and, she, then,* and *it*—and non-standard spelling—*wun* (one), *grl* (girl), *sed* (said), and *rabt* (rabbit). She is using her knowledge of phonics to sound out words she does not know how to spell.

Her writing uses book language containing speech, as in this example: "She sed don't." (*She said, "Don't."*) She appears influenced by repetitive patterned stories

---

through the use of a repeated phrase: She said, *"Poo, poo." The horse bucked her off and she said, "Hoppy, Hoppy." The rabbit bit her finger.*

The story begins in an expected way, "One day..." and follows a pattern. The story appears to be continuing even at the end, suggesting Erin may have more to add. She shows that she understands what a word is by leaving spaces in between. There is no punctuation as yet in her writing. This sample indicates that Erin is an emergent writer with a developing understanding of how language works.

Teachers may find it helpful to use a modified version of the evaluation criteria used for provincial, state, or nation-wide achievement tests (figure 5.2.).

EVALUATION OF ERIN'S WRITING SAMPLE

Content	Vocabulary
• Story follows a repetitive pattern of a little girl who meets two animals, first a horse, then a rabbit. • Story appears interrupted or unfinished at the end.	• Erin uses book language in her story (i.e., "One day..." and "She said..."). • Erin appears to use language that is part of her speaking vocabulary, rather than using vocabulary she might find easy to spell.
Sentence Structure	**Conventions**
• Erin uses compound sentences, where *and* is used to combine two ideas. • Erin uses the word *then* to show story sequence.	• Erin uses both standard and non-standard spelling. • Erin uses her knowledge of phonics to sound out unfamiliar words. • Erin is not yet using punctuation in her writing.

Reproducible master in appendix T.

Figure 5.2. Examples of evaluation criteria.

ANECDOTAL OBSERVATIONS

Using anecdotal observations, teachers keep track of students' habits, developmental levels, and writing strategies during writers workshop. This method of documenting ensures not only a record of students' writing products, but also a record of student writing processes—teacher observations are based on actual practice.

Teachers make many different kinds of observations. Some of these include:

- effort and involvement in writing
- progress from the previous day's or week's writing
- use of language (using more interesting vocabulary or longer sentences)
- risk-taking in writing about new topics
- use of time
- involvement in stages of the writing process

Many primary teachers use 3 ½" x 5" recipe cards to record their observations during, or immediately after, writers workshop. Others create their own anecdotal worksheets to use (see the example of anecdotal recordkeeping in figure 5.3).

Marissa	Tom	**Joshua**	**April 12**
Emily	Joshua		
Michael	Connor		

For the Joshua card:

Joshua   **April 12**

- Today Joshua worked very hard on his story about working on the farm with his dad.
- More standard spelling than in previous stories.
- Still having trouble with *they*—spells it "thay."
- Is trying out quotation marks in this story.

Reproducible master in appendix U.

Figure 5.3. Example of anecdotal recordkeeping.

STUDENT SELF-ASSESSMENT

Even students in the primary grades can learn to talk about their writing and about themselves as writers. For example, at various times throughout the year ask students to think about how their writing has improved. In a whole-group mini-lesson, record their answers on chart paper and categorize their responses under the headings of:

- **Language use** • A student may respond, "I am using more interesting words in my writing now."

- **Conventions** • A student may respond, "I am using capitals on names and for places in my writing."

- **Sentence structure** • A student may respond, "I join some of my sentences together using *and* or *because*."

- **Content** • A student may respond, "I am writing about things that I like to learn about and so my stories are more interesting."

These discussions introduce young students to the process of self-evaluation and to evaluation criteria for writing. Ask students to write about how they think their writing has improved throughout the school year. Figure 5.4 shows two examples of student self-assessment.

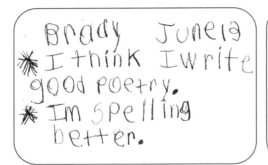

Brady Juneia
❋ I think I write
good Poetry.
❋ Im spelling
better.

❋ I think that I inproved on spelling
more words corectly.

❋ I think that I inproved on
writing more intresting stories.

I wish that I didn't use
said so much.

Figure 5.4. Examples of two students' self-assessments. A grade-one student wrote the assessment on the left. The assessment on the right is by a grade-two student.

STUDENT INTERVIEWS

On two or three occasions throughout the school year, it is helpful to conduct short (five to ten minute) interviews with students about their perceptions of writing. The interviews can be done during conferences or at other times throughout the day. For kindergarten and grade-one students, the interview is best conducted orally using a sample of the student's own writing as a starting point. Grade-two and grade-three students can fill out a short questionnaire about writing, and bring this to the interview to discuss with you.

A short interview can yield significant insight into a writer. The interview gives you a glimpse into how a young student thinks about learning to write. For instance, if a student says she likes writing because it is "peaceful and quiet," find ways to

Figure 5.5. An example of a writer's profile—celebrating student writing.

provide a quiet place where this student may write. Interviews can help you decide how best to help the writer. See appendix K for questions you can use to guide the interview.

CREATING A WRITER'S PROFILE

A writer's profile is a "snapshot" of the student writer at a particular time in his or her development. It is often made up of a short interview with the student, a sample of his or her writing, a photograph of the student, and observations made by the teacher and/or parents about the student's writing. Teachers can display these profiles on bulletin boards in the school or give each student an individual profile to take home. The profile lets each student "see" him- or herself as a writer in a positive way.

REPORTING TO PARENTS

Parents can be a resource for the writing classroom. They may be invited into the classroom to listen to students read their writing, to assist with self-evaluation and editing, to help students find books and other research material for their writing, and to help publish student writing in a variety of ways.

Send home a letter at the beginning of the year to give parents an overview of the writing program and your goals, and suggest ways that parents can help their children develop as writers (appendix M).

SUMMARY

- Most teachers give impoverished responses to students' writing.

- Assessment is the act of observing carefully and thoughtfully, while evaluation is the interpretation of those observations in relation to curriculum expectations or other forms of quality indicators.

- Student self-assessment can take the form of checklists, interviews, and goal setting.

- Reporting to parents is an essential component of writing assessment and evaluation.

- Teachers assess writing competency through observation, anecdotal records, checklists, writing samples, student self-assessments, and writing profiles.

NOTES

APPENDICES

THE WRITING PROCESS

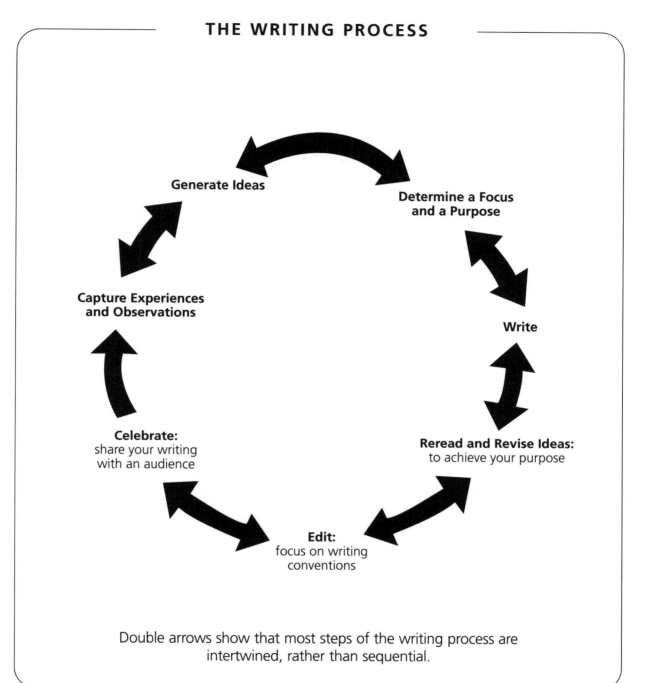

Generate Ideas

Determine a Focus
and a Purpose

Write

Reread and Revise Ideas:
to achieve your purpose

Edit:
focus on writing
conventions

Celebrate:
share your writing
with an audience

Capture Experiences
and Observations

Double arrows show that most steps of the writing process are
intertwined, rather than sequential.

A DEVELOPMENTAL CONTINUUM FOR PRESCHOOL WRITING

AGE GROUP	WRITING DEVELOPMENT
Before age 3	Children produce mostly random scribbling.
Around age 3	Children begin to understand some of the things that writing is used for (e.g., "This is a letter for Grandma," or "I've written a list of things to buy when we go shopping"). Some children also begin to understand that writing consists of letter-like formations (although they can't necessarily name the letters produced).
Around age 4	Students' awareness of letters becomes more specific. For instance, students can often name letters in their own names or point out the big letter *M* for McDonald's. After producing letters, they will often tell another person what it says. There will likely be no attempt to sound out the letters. However, what they have written may look like a story or a message. Some students will bring their "writing" to an adult and ask, "What does it say?"
Between ages 5 and 7	Students discover that print represents the sounds of words. Some students make this discovery in kindergarten. Other students are not aware that print represents the sounds of words until well into grade one. It is important to keep in mind that although students first produce scribbles, pictures, and letters, their understanding proceeds from sentences, to words, and finally to letters. Their scribbles can be used to represent any of these (Casbergue, 1998).

WRITING INSTRUCTION SURVEY

1. How many years of teaching experience do you have? _____
   At which grade levels? _____
   What subjects have you taught?

   _____

   _____

   _____

2. In your university teacher education, did you receive instruction in the teaching of writing? If so, please describe.

   _____

   _____

   _____

   _____

3. Was there anything you found particularly valuable in your studies about teaching writing? Was there anything lacking?

   _____

   _____

   _____

   _____

4. (a) If you have time and opportunity, do you write for pleasure? Have you done so in the past? Please describe.

   _____

   _____

   _____

   (b) Do you ever share your own writing with your students? Please describe.

   _____

   _____

   _____

5. If you were asked to characterize your writing program for another teacher, what would you say? What would you emphasize?

   _____

   _____

   _____

6. What are your goals in helping students to write? What do you want your students to take away with them at the end of the year concerning their writing? Please specify.

   _____

   _____

   _____

(cont'd)

7. (a) What kinds of skills do you work on in writing?

_____

_____

_____

(b) What kinds of attitudes do you hope students will have about writing when they leave your classroom?

_____

_____

_____

_____

_____

8. What do you do to help students find topics to write about?

_____

_____

_____

_____

9. What frustrates you the most about teaching writing to your students?

_____

_____

_____

_____

10. What writing activities have proven most successful for you and your students? Why?

_____

_____

_____

11. Think of a student who has impressed you as being a good writer. How would you describe him or her and the writing he or she produces?

_____

_____

_____

_____

12. Any additional comments you'd like to add about the teaching of writing:

_____

_____

_____

_____

_____

PRINCIPLES FOR MANAGING TIME

1. Encourage students to develop fluency in their writing by helping them to seek out "standard" spellings on word walls, in their individualized spelling books, and from peers.

2. Encourage students to draw pictures, scribble lines, or sound out the words to the best of their ability when they use vocabulary in their writing that they cannot find in the above places. For example, a student attempting to write the word *especially* might write "espvvvv" or "esphesle."

3. Keep track of individual student's writing progress by creating a "tracking" sheet. At the beginning of writers workshop, students write their names under the appropriate headings—prewriting, drafting, revising/editing, publishing, conferencing—to indicate what they are working on that day.

4. Develop routines that students can carry out on their own. For example, student helpers distribute writing folders during recess or at lunch. Students assemble themselves on a carpeted area of the classroom in preparation for the mini-lesson that begins writers workshop.

PRINCIPLES FOR REVISING

1. Focus on helping students engage in writing for real purposes. One example of this is the "sign-in" routine. Kindergarten students learn the value of writing by signing an attendance page each day. The routine helps them to practice and experiment with letter shape and size, spelling, and with viewing other's efforts.

2. Focus mostly on drafting during the writing process. This allows students to develop fluency and independence.

3. Teach the *habit* of revising as much as the *actual* revision. Researchers call this "monitoring their own writing behaviors" and suggest students do this when they are encouraged to be active in learning.

4. Judge each revision situation according to the student. Since it is unlikely that any writer attempts to revise all aspects of a piece of writing at one time, it does not make sense for a student to do this. As a rule of thumb, limit the student's number of revisions to between three and five on a single page (depending on the student's ability to handle these).

CLASSROOM	WORKSHOP

ROUTINES FOR WRITERS WORKSHOP

- **Mini-lessons**—short focused lessons most often directed by the teacher on some aspect of writing and/or writers workshop

- **Writing folders or booklets**—folders maintained by the students containing topics for writing, writing in progress, and published pieces

- **Quiet writing time**—classroom time devoted to students engaged in their writing

- **Conferencing (teacher-led or student-led)**—meetings between students or between the teacher and individual students to discuss aspects of a piece of writing

- **Author's circle**—a place where students can share writing in progress or published writing in a supportive environment

- **Editing table**—a table where students can take their writing to when they engage in the processes of revision and editing

- **Celebration or publication opportunities**—formal and informal opportunities for students to show and share their writing with an audience

- **Word wall**—a large chart or bulletin board that organizes new vocabulary for students as an aid to writing and spelling

- **Individual spelling books**—booklets containing high-frequency words for spelling as well as words requested and used by the student (maintained throughout the year by the student and the teacher)

- **Status-of-the-class checklist**—a form of recordkeeping used by the teacher to keep track of the writing done by students, processes engaged in, and problems encountered (appendix I)

- **Writing record (students)**—a form maintained by the student indicating the pieces written, including dates begun and completed (appendix J)

- **Writers' survey**—a list of questions posed orally (by the teacher) or on paper to find out about a student's perceptions of, and attitudes toward, writing (appendix K)

QUESTIONS & COMMENTS FOR USE WITH YOUNG STUDENTS WHILE CONFERENCING

1. Before you begin, tell me about your piece.

2. Please read your piece to me.

3. What is your favorite sentence?

4. Who would you like to give this piece of writing to?

5. As you are reading, could you do some editing, too? Put in periods and upper case letters?

6. Is there anything you want to add to or change about this piece?

7. Where did you get the idea for this piece?

8. Do you have questions about this piece of writing?

9. _____

_____

10. _____

_____

11. _____

_____

12. _____

_____

13. _____

_____

14. _____

_____

STATUS-OF-THE-CLASS CHECKLIST

KEY			
D: Drafting	**R/E:** Revising/Editing	**C:** Conferencing	**PW:** Prewriting

Name	Date						
1.							
2.							
3.							
4.							
5.							
6.							
7.							
8.							
9.							
10.							
11.							
12.							
13.							
14.							
15.							
16.							
17.							
18.							
19.							
20.							
21.							
22.							
23.							
24.							
25.							
26.							
27.							
28.							
29.							
30.							

WRITING RECORD

Student's Name			
Date Writing Begun	Title	Form	Date Completed
1.			
2.			
3.			
4.			
5.			
6.			
7.			
8.			
9.			
10.			
11.			
12.			
13.			
14.			
15.			
16.			
17.			
18.			
19.			
20.			

WRITER'S SURVEY

1. Do you like to write? _____

2. What do you like to write about? _____
   _____

3. Do you like to write first and then illustrate, or do you like to illustrate first and
   then write? _____
   _____

4. Is writing sometimes hard for you? _____

5. What makes it hard? _____
   _____

6. Is writing sometimes easy for you?_____

7. What makes it easy? _____
   _____

8. Which piece of writing is your best so far this year? _____
   _____

9. What makes it your best? _____
   _____

10. What advice do you have for someone who is having a hard time with writing?
    _____

11. Do you like writing "real" stories or made-up stories? Why?_____
    _____

12. Is there something that I do to help you with writing? What is it? _____
    _____
    _____

13. What do you need to learn in order to become an even better writer than you
    are now? _____
    _____

14. If you woke up tomorrow morning and everything was the same except for one
    thing—you could not write anymore—would it matter to you? _____
    _____

15. _____
    _____
    _____

WEEKLY SIGN-IN SHEET

Teacher's Model	Monday	Tuesday	Wednesday	Thursday	Friday

Dear Parents and/or Guardians:

This school year the students will be learning to write during a special time set aside twice a week, called "Writers Workshop."

At the beginning of the year, I will help students make a list of topics they can choose to write about. This list will be updated throughout the year, but your suggestions about family activities would also be helpful. In this way, students will learn to write independently on topics they choose themselves.

We will work on writing skills such as spelling, punctuation, and grammar during each Writers Workshop in a mini-lesson at the beginning of class. I will give each student individual instruction at conferences that will be held in class. Students will be encouraged to share their finished pieces with the class while seated in the author's chair. You are most welcome to come and listen to your child read his or her writing.

From time to time, guest authors and illustrators will visit our classroom to talk to the students about writing and to provide assistance to the students. Your assistance during Writers Workshop would also be appreciated throughout the year. You could assist by:

- listening to students read their stories
- making booklets for students to publish their stories in
- typing students' writing on the computer
- taking students to the library to find books related to their writing
- conferencing with your own child about his or her writing

Writers Workshop is a well-established approach to teaching writing that is flexible enough to meet a variety of students' needs and interests. I am looking forward to helping students develop as writers using this approach.

Please feel free to contact me if you would like to volunteer in our classroom or if you have any comments or questions you would like to discuss. Thank you.

Sincerely,

HOME AND SCHOOL JOURNAL

Date: _____

1. Student's message to teacher	2. Teacher's response
3. Student's message to parent/guardian	**4. Parent/guardian's response**

K-W-L STRATEGY

TOPIC: _____

What do I know?	What do I want to know?	What have I learned?

VENN DIAGRAM—COMPARING AND CONTRASTING

VENN DIAGRAM—COMPARING AND CONTRASTING

REPORT-WRITING CHART

CONCEPT MAP

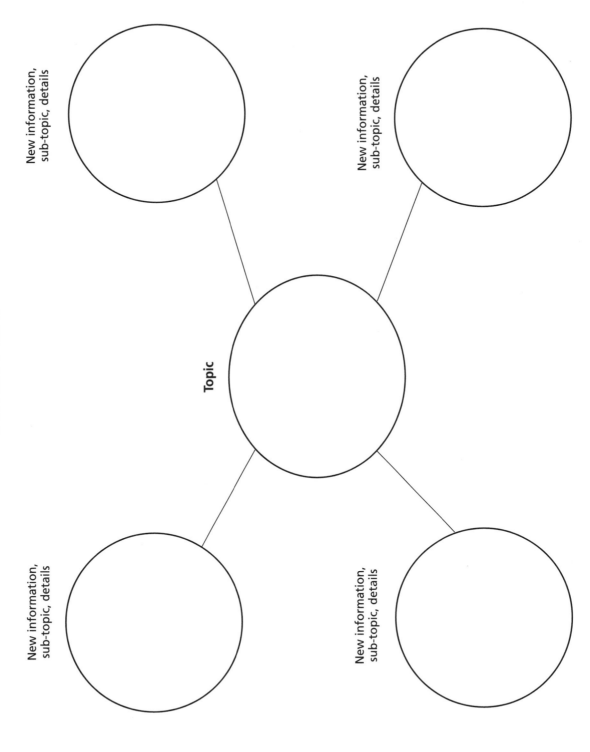

New information, sub-topic, details

New information, sub-topic, details

Topic

New information, sub-topic, details

New information, sub-topic, details

EVALUATION

Student's Name _____

Content	Vocabulary

Sentence Structure	Conventions

- -

Student's Name _____

Content	Vocabulary

Sentence Structure	Conventions

ANECDOTAL RECORD

Student's Name	Date
Comments:	

Student's Name	Date
Comments:	

Student's Name	Date
Comments:	

Student's Name	Date
Comments:	

Student's Name	Date
Comments:	

Student's Name	Date
Comments:	

REFERENCES

Askew, B., & Fountas, I. (1998). Building an early reading process: Active from the start! *The Reading Teacher*, Vol. 52(2), 126–137.

Atwell, N. (1997). *In the middle: Writing, reading, and learning with adolescents.* Upper Montclair, NJ: Boynton/Cook Publishers.

_____. (1999). *In the middle: New understandings about writing, reading, and learning* (2nd ed.). Portsmouth, NH: Boynton/Cook Publishers.

Bright, R. (1995). *Writing instruction in the intermediate grades: What is said, what is done, what is understood.* Newark, DE: International Reading Association.

Bright, R., McMullin, L., & Platt, D. (1998). *From your child's teacher: Helping your child learn to read, write, and speak.* Edmonton, AB: FP Hendriks Publishing.

Calkins, L. (1991). Mini-lessons: An overview, and tools to help teachers create their own mini-lessons. In B. Miller Power and R. Hubbard (Eds.), *Literacy in process* (pp. 149–173). Portsmouth, NH: Heinemann.

Cameron, L. (1998). A Practitioner's Reflections. ORBIT: *A Commentary on the World of Education*, Vol. 28(4), 10–16.

Casbergue, R. (1998). How do we foster young children's writing development? In S. Neuman & K. Roskos (Eds.), *Children achieving: Best practices in early literacy* (pp. 198–222). Newark, DE: International Reading Association.

Clay, M. (1975). *What did I write?* Portsmouth, NH: Heinemann.

_____. (1993). *An observation survey: Of early literacy achievement.* Portsmouth, NH: Heinemann.

Dahl, K., & Farnan, N. (1998). *Student's writing: Perspectives from research.* Newark, DE: International Reading Association.

Dyson, A. Haas. (1989). *Multiple worlds of child writers: Friends learning to write.* New York, NY: Teachers College Press.

Ede, L. (1995). *Work in progress: A guide to writing and revising.* New York, NY: St. Martin's Press.

Elbow, P. (1993). *The uses of binary thinking. Journal of Advanced Composition*, 13(1), 237–348.

_____. (2000). *Everyone can write.* New York, NY: Oxford University Press.

Fitch, S. (1995). *I am small.* Toronto, ON: Doubleday.

Goldberg, N. (1986). *Writing down the bones: Freeing the writer within.* Boston: Shambhala.

Goodman, K. (1986). *What's whole in whole language?* Portsmouth, NH: Heinemann.

Graves, D. (1982). *Writing: teachers and children at work.* Portsmouth, NH: Heinemann.

_____. (1991). All children can write. In B. Power & R. Hubbard (Eds.), *Literacy in Process*, (pp. 67–78). Portsmouth, NH: Heinemann.

Hall, N. (1998). Real literacy in a school setting: Five-year olds take on the world. *The Reading Teacher*, 52(1), 8–17.

Harste, J., Woodward, V., & Burke, C. (1991). Examining instructional assumptions. In B. Power & R. Hubbard (Eds.), *Literacy in process* (pp. 51–66). Portsmouth, NH: Heinemann.

Hiebert, E., & Raphael, T. (1998). *Early literacy instruction.* Orlando, FL: Harcourt Brace & Company.

Hillocks, G. (1986). *Research on written communications: New directions for teaching.* New York, NY: NCRE.

Howard, E. Fitzgerald. (1995). *Aunt Flossie's Hats and Crab Cakes Later.* Boston, MA: Clarion Books.

Jackson, N., & Pillow, P. (1999). *The reading-writing workshop* (Grades 1–5). New York, NY: Scholastic.

Johnson, T. and Johnson, D. (1990). *Bringing it all together: A program for literacy.* Richmond Hill, ON: Scholastic.

Krogness, M. M. (1987). Folklore: A matter of the heart and the heart of the matter. *Language Arts*, 64, 808–818.

Language across the curriculum. (1992). Toronto, ON: Houghton Mifflin.

Morrow, L., Tracey, D., & Pressley, M. (1999). Characteristics of exemplary first-grade literacy instruction. *The Reading Teacher*, Vol. 25(5), 462–476.

Murray, D. (1990). *Shop talk: Learning to write with writers.* Portsmouth, NH: Boynton/Cook Publishers.

_____. (1991). Getting under the lightning. In B. Miller Power & R. Hubbard (Eds.), *Literacy in process* (pp. 5–13). Portsmouth, NH: Heinemann.

Newman, J. (1984). *The craft of children's writing.* New York, NY: Scholastic.

Ogle, D. (1986). K-W-L: A teacher model that develops active reading of expository text. *The Reading Teacher*, Vol. 39, 564–570.

Peterson, S. (1995). *Becoming better writers*. Edmonton, AB: FP Hendriks Publishing.

Picciotto, L. (2002). Emergent literacy pro-file. In G. Tompkins, et. al. (Eds.), *Language arts: Content and teaching strategies* (pp. 134–135). Toronto, ON: Pearson Education Canada.

Richgels, D., Poremba, K., & McGee, L. (1996). Kindergarteners talk about print: Phonemic awareness in meaningful contexts. *The Reading Teacher*, Vol. 49(8), 632–645.

Rief, L. (1989). Seeking diversity: Reading and writing from the middle to the edge. In N. Atwell (Ed.), *Workshop by and for teachers* (pp. 13–24). Portsmouth, NH: Heinemann.

Rief, L., & Atwell, N. (1991). *Seeking diversity: Language arts with adolescents*. Portsmouth, NH: Heinemann.

Romano, T. (1987). *Clearing the way: Working with teenage writers*. Portsmouth, NH: Heinemann.

Rosenblatt, L. (1978). *The reader, the text, the poem: The transactional theory of the literary work*. Carbondale, IL: Southern Illinois Press.

Rylant, C. (1985). *The relatives came*. New York, NY: Simon & Schuster Children's Publishing.

Short, K. (1995). *Research & professional resources in children's literature: Piecing a patchwork quilt*. Newark, DL: International Reading Association.

Short, K., Harste, J., & Burke, C. (1996). *Creating classrooms for authors and inquirers*. (2nd Ed.). Portsmouth, NH: Heinemann.

Smith, F. (1982). *Writing and the writer*. New York, NY: Holt, Rhinehart and Winston.

Stanovich, P. (1998). Shaping practice to fit the evidence. *ORBIT: A Commentary on the World of Education*, Vol. 28(4), 37–43.

Teale, W., & Sulzby, E. (1986). *Emergent literacy: Writing & reading*. Norwood, NJ: Ablex.

Tompkins, G., Bright, R., Pollard, M., & Winsor, P. (2002). *Language arts: Content & teaching strategies*. Toronto, ON: Pearson Education.

Vygotsky, L. (1978). *Thought and language*. Cambridge, MA: MIT Press.

Walton, M., Staley, M., & Fox, A. (1999). *This is about a fight: Stories of violence by central city school children*. Paper presented at the Biennial Meeting of the Society for Research in Child Development, Albuquerque, NM.

Wells, G. (1986). *The meaning makers: Children learning language and using language to learn*. Portsmouth, NH: Heinemann.

_____. (1998). Interview with Gordon Wells. Talking about phonics. *ORBIT: A Commentary on the World of Education*, Vol 28(4), 4–6.